MILLION DOLLAR ACTION

A **WE SHOULD ALL BE MILLIONAIRES** WORKBOOK

Your Step-by-Step Guide to Making Wealth Happen

RACHEL RODGERS

HARPERCOLLINS
LEADERSHIP

AN IMPRINT OF HARPERCOLLINS

Published by HarperCollins Leadership, an imprint
of HarperCollins Focus LLC.

ISBN 978-1-4002-5172-8 (eBook)

ISBN 978-1-4002-4368-6 (TP)

Library of Congress Cataloging-in-Publication Data
*Library of Congress Cataloging-in-Publication application
has been submitted.*

Printed in the United States of America

24 25 26 27 28 LBC 6 5 4 3 2

To the ambitious ones.

The ones that know they are meant for more.

The ones that know they haven't reached their full potential yet.

The ones that are tired of being underestimated . . .

and tired of underestimating themselves.

And to the ones who are ready to take action.

I see you.

This one is for you.

xo,

R

CONTENTS

FOREWORD

Dear Reader,

My debut book, *We Should All Be Millionaires: A Woman's Guide to Earning More, Building Wealth, and Gaining Economic Power*, was released in May 2021 by HarperCollins Leadership. It became an instant bestseller and I have been overjoyed by the response to it. The book sold over 100,000 copies in its first year and continues to sell. It has been chosen for countless book clubs and garnered a great deal of national media coverage. While all of that is very exciting, nothing compares to the many messages I have received from readers like you who have read the book and taken action.

So many readers have written to me to tell me about the Million Dollar Boundaries they set, the Million Dollar Decisions they've made, and the Million Dollar Squad they've assembled. I've learned about higher salaries negotiated and new businesses launched. And so many readers have conducted their very own $10k in 10 Days Challenge with much success. I could not be more proud of all of the action you have taken.

My message in *We Should All Be Millionaires* is bold and direct: You could be earning vastly more than you currently do; you should aim for an income of seven figures per year, not six; and your life will be significantly better once you have more money in your pocket.

In the book, I shared my personal story of becoming a self-made millionaire while raising four children. I told the story of how I climbed from crushing debt and financial stress to wealth and abundance, running a multimillion-dollar company and living a joyful, peaceful life with my family on my own terms.

My goal is to inspire you, the reader, to construct a new attitude about money, claim your power, and build the financial security that you need and deserve.

Because, for too long, women, people of color, queer folks, and other systemically marginalized communities have been trapped in a financial prison—under-earning, struggling to make ends meet, just barely getting by. It's time for us to make more money and build serious wealth, so that we can stop merely surviving and start thriving.

I love all of the action my dear readers have taken toward this goal. And I know by your many messages that you are ready for more. I created this book to help you take specific, effective action toward your goal of becoming a millionaire. The steps that I will walk you through in this workbook were previously only available to my entrepreneur clients. I am making them available to you because I want to help you achieve your goals faster and with more efficiency and joy.

Let's start building your bank account right now.

xo,
Rachel

INTRODUCTION

WHY YOU NEED MORE MONEY

I was on a business trip—2,467 miles away from home—when I got the call, the kind of phone call you never want to receive. Every mother's worst nightmare.

I heard my husband on the other end of the line, babbling, speaking rapidly, and crying.

In more than eleven years of marriage, I've heard my husband cry maybe once or twice. This was not normal.

Immediately, my mama instincts fired off. Something had happened. Something terrible.

"The ambulance is on its way," I heard him say. "Jackson had a seizure."

Our son was experiencing a febrile seizure, although we didn't know the official terminology at the time. As we later learned from the hospital staff, it's a seizure brought on by a fever and most often happens to small children. While it tends to be brief and relatively harmless, it looks absolutely terrifying. Severe shaking. Loss of consciousness. It's a moment that makes a parent's heart stop.

Our baby had no previous history of seizures. Nothing like this had ever happened before. My husband was petrified and feared the worst. So did I.

In that moment, standing in my hotel room with my phone in my hand, my husband sobbing, and ambulance sirens blaring in the background, all I could think was:

I need to be home with my baby. Right now.

Hurling clothes into my suitcase, I booked a super-last-minute flight back home. Options were limited, and with three layovers, the flight ended up costing $2,000. Expensive? Yes. Overpriced? Probably. But I paid without a moment's hesitation. It wasn't even a question. It was a must-do.

I got home as rapidly as possible and reunited with my family. To my huge relief, everything was okay and, soon, Jackson was cleared to leave the hospital.

Once things had calmed down and all the kids were tucked into bed, I took a deep breath (and settled my nerves with a just-survived-a-living-nightmare glass of wine) and reflected on the events that had just transpired.

I had a sobering realization.

If this crisis had happened ten years ago, I realized, I would not have been able to buy that expensive plane ticket and come home as quickly as I did. I would not have been able to afford it.

Which means I would have been forced to wait. For hours. Maybe days. Trying to rustle the money together, or trying to find a cheaper way back home, something I could afford. If Jackson cried out for his mama, I wouldn't have been there. And if his situation had been worse . . .

It was too painful to even finish the thought.

You see, ten years earlier, I was in a very different financial situation: maxed out credit cards. Low (often below zero) balance in my checking account. Overdraft fines. Living paycheck to paycheck. Crushed by student loan debt. No health insurance. Barely scraping by.

Even though I was working full-time (more than full-time, actually) my $41,000 salary as a judicial clerk for a state judge didn't stretch very far. Money was always tighter than a pair of maximum strength Spanx.

Ten years earlier, I simply did not have the ability to spontaneously purchase a $2,000 plane ticket at a moment's notice. I barely had the ability to purchase a spontaneous $15 Caesar chicken salad without nervously checking my online banking app on my phone (covertly, under the lunch table) to make sure the card would go through and I wouldn't see that shame-inducing word: declined.

If Jackson's seizure had happened ten years earlier, I would have been trapped. Literally trapped, imprisoned, pacing frantically back and forth like a rat in a cage, thousands of miles from home, unable to go to my baby in the hospital due to financial limitations. A horrendous situation.

Yet millions of people find themselves in some version of this scenario every single day. Wanting (or needing) to do something, but unable to do it, due to lack of funds.

Dear Reader:

This is why you need to have more money.

It's for moments like these.

You need more money so that you can swipe your card and buy an emergency plane ticket whenever you need to, without a second thought.

You need more money so that you can get the very best food, housing, education, mental and physical healthcare for yourself and the people you love.

You need more money so that you can write a phat check to a progressive political candidate that you admire, a rising star who's changing the world for the better.

Having more money is never really about "the money."

It's about the people you love and the causes you care about.

It's about having more options instead of being limited to the worst options on the menu.

It's about having the power to do whatever you want or need to do.

And, yes, having more money is also about beauty, inspiration, joy, and pleasure—all of which are your birthright as a human being. Having the ability to take your family on an unforgettable vacation and go kayaking in the ocean, treat yourself to rose-scented body oil, and enjoy a beautiful quality of life.

Listen closely:

I never want you to be in a situation where you feel trapped, powerless, abused, or exhausted simply because you don't have enough money. I never want you to be in that position. Ever again. That is why I wrote my book, *We Should All Be Millionaires*, and this companion workbook.

If you are determined to earn more money and change your financial situation, then you are in the right place, and you are definitely holding the right book.

We will begin with a brief definition (what is a "millionaire," exactly?). Then we'll discuss a few uncomfortable facts about money and some of the biggest myths about money. And then we'll dive into your first set of action steps.

This journey is going to be emotionally challenging at times, but also invigorating, exciting, and full of hope.

I hope you have a pot of coffee brewing and a pen ready, because I am about to put you to work!

MILLION DOLLAR QUESTION

Can you remember a time when you couldn't do something that you really needed or wanted to do, simply because you didn't have enough money to do it?

Maybe it happened ten years ago. Or ten minutes ago.

What happened? How did you feel? What did you learn from that experience? Take a moment to reflect. Write down what you remember. Or talk it out with a friend.

_____

_____

_____

_____

_____

_____

_____

_____

_____

_____

_____

_____

Repeat these words: "That is never going to happen in my life. Never. Ever. Again."

WHAT IS A MILLIONAIRE, EXACTLY?

While reading *We Should All Be Millionaires: A Woman's Guide to Earning More, Building Wealth, and Gaining Economic Power*, and working through this companion workbook, you may wonder:

- When you say "millionaire," what do you mean exactly? How do you define that term?

- When you say, "We should all be millionaires," do you mean that literally? Do you mean, all 3.9 billion women on Earth should be millionaires? Or is this statement more of a metaphor?

Personally, I define a millionaire as someone who has a seven-figure net worth. This means at least $1,000,000 in assets, which may include cash in the bank, investments, a profitable business (yes, your business is an asset), and other things that you own: real estate, cars, boats, fine art, land, and so on.

Some people define a millionaire as someone whose personal income or salary is seven figures per year. And some would say a millionaire is someone who is running a company that generates seven figures or more in annual revenue.

Pick whatever definition you prefer. The point is that a millionaire is someone who is financially secure, abundant, prosperous, who is maximizing his or her earning potential (instead of leaving cash on the table), and who has vast options in life instead of being limited.

When I say, "We should all be millionaires," what I mean is that every woman[1] should have financial security and economic power. And every woman deserves to live free of financial stress.

---

[1] *We Should All Be Millionaires* was originally written for women. However, many readers—including male people of color, queer men, trans folks, non-binary folks, immigrants, disabled people, plus size people, anyone and everyone who is part of a marginalized community—have read and benefited from the book. For the sake of ease in writing, I will continue to refer to women throughout the book, but please know that if you do not identify as a woman, but are a member of another historically and systemically marginalized community, this book is for you, too.

I understand, of course, that not every woman wants to become a millionaire.

For instance, some women want to clock into a job, clock out, go home, and don't want the responsibilities that many millionaires contend with, such as building a company, hiring, firing, nurturing a team, or being in the public eye. Some women are content with having less cash and can still experience freedom, peace, and joy on a modest budget. If that's true for you, that's fine.

However, my stance is that every woman *could* be earning more than she currently does. And every woman who wants to become a millionaire *should* pursue this goal unapologetically and *can* achieve it.

If you are truly satisfied with having less money, that's cool. It's your life. Do what feels right. Maybe you'd like to become a "mini-naire" with a smaller net worth. A few hundred thousand, perhaps, but not necessarily millions. If that's what you really want, you can create it.

But . . .

I challenge you to dream bigger and get fiercely honest with yourself.

Is it really true that you don't want or need more money? Or is this something you're telling yourself because you're afraid to want more?

Are you afraid of failing? Afraid of disappointing yourself and others? Perhaps it feels safer to want less rather than allow yourself to want more.

Maybe, deep down, becoming a seven-figure badass is something you absolutely want. I suspect that it is. You were attracted to this particular book (with "million" in the title) for a reason. It's time to own your ambitions instead of pretending they do not exist.

Our society routinely tells women: "Be satisfied with less. Make do. Eat less. Earn less. Take up less space." I am here to tell you the exact opposite. Earn the most. Be the most. Unleash your inner millionaire.

THE UNCOMFORTABLE FACTS ABOUT MONEY

This workbook is filled with action steps for you to complete, but first, let's look at the uncomfortable facts about you and your cash. Know the facts before you do the work.

We live in a world that is outrageously imbalanced when it comes to women, queer folks, people of color, those with disabilities, and other systemically marginalized communities.

In our world today, heterosexual, cisgender, white men hold the lion's share of the world's wealth. Women and other marginalized groups are left with the smallest of crumbs. Flakes at the bottom of the croissant tray.

A few statistics you need to know:

- 90 percent of the world's millionaires are men. Only 10 percent are women. This statistic pretty much says it all. We're at 90–10, folks. Not even remotely close to 50–50. We have work to do. Good thing you're holding this book in your hands.

- 13 percent of men earn $100,000 and more per year. Only 6 percent of women earn that much. Ouch.

- Women are 80 percent more likely than men to be impoverished in retirement. No surprise there. When you are underpaid your entire life, of course you're going to end up in a precarious financial situation in your senior years.

- On average, a Black household in America has a net worth of about $17,000. For a white household, $170,000. Literally ten times more.

- For women who work in a corporate setting, only one in five people with high-paying, executive positions are women, and only one in twenty-five are women of color. Those of you who work at large companies, I can feel you nodding your head. You've seen it.

- There are more than 12 million woman-owned companies in the United States today. Hooray! Except, here comes a soggy towel to cover that celebratory cake, because the financial picture is not good.

- Out of those 12 million woman-owned companies, the majority (78 percent) remain financially stuck, never generating more than $50,000 per year in annual revenue.

- A tiny minority (4 percent) of those woman-owned companies will thrive financially and generate $500,000 to $1,000,000 per year, and more.

- These statistics paint a clear picture, and it's not cute.

Across the board, regardless of your profession—whether you work for an employer or run your own company—women tend to earn significantly less than men.

Do these stats anger you? Do you feel disgusted, infuriated, sad, or numb? Those are all perfectly valid and understandable responses.

Feel whatever you feel. Cry, rage, scream into a pillow. And then, harness those emotions and use them as fuel.

Write down what you are feeling as you consider the fact that you have been underpaid and under-earning. Journaling is a great way to process your feelings.

Let those emotions motivate you to do the work that is required to change your financial situation and our society as well. Your future can be radically different from your present and past.

THE BIGGEST MYTHS ABOUT MONEY

I want you to successfully complete all the action steps in this workbook. But first, we need to "take out the mind trash."

This means we need to identify thoughts in your head that are absolute trash—myths, misconceptions, limiting beliefs, mental blocks that are hindering your progress.

Because, if your head is stuffed full of mind trash, then you will feel hopeless and exhausted, and you will struggle to get moving and do the work that needs to be done.

Beep, beep. You hear that? It's garbage pick-up day and here comes the truck. Put those bins on the curb!

Let's bust a few of the biggest and most insidious myths about money.

MYTH:

"The best way to become wealthy is to stop buying your daily latte, stop getting takeout, stop all those frivolous luxuries, and start making your own soap out of tree bark. Cut back on spending, ladies!"

Absolutely false.

This statement is ludicrous and insulting. It also doesn't make any rational sense. Just look at the math.

If you stop buying your daily latte, you will save $5 a day, which is $1,825 per year. If you tuck those savings away every year, it would take you more than (take a deep breath) 547 years to save $1,000,000.

You're going to be waiting a long-ass time for all those latte dollars to add up. In 547 years, you will be a petrified mummy in a sarcophagus.

Even if you invested that $1,825 into an index fund annually with an 8% rate of return, it would still take 50 years for it to turn into $1,000,000. I don't know about you, but when I was struggling to make ends meet I did not want to wait 50 years to experience financial well-being.

Many so-called financial experts bark at women and insist: "Stop slurping down those pumpkin spice lattes, you self-indulgent fool! Cut back on daily indulgences and you'll be swimming in cash." But this is not an efficient path to wealth. This is a joke.

Instead of telling women and girls, "You need to scrimp and save and eliminate all pleasure from your life so that you can save $2,000 per year," we need to change the conversation.

We need to teach women how to earn an additional $2,000 *per week,* and then $3,000, and then $5,000, and beyond. Now *that* is a far more exciting conversation.

Invest your precious time and mental energy into activities that *generate more money.*

Instead of spending hours trying to figure out how to shave $100 off your annual phone bill, you could spend that time launching a side hustle, negotiating a raise, or contacting potential clients to pitch your services to bring $10,000 in the door.

Do you want to save $100 this month, or earn $10,000? Which option would make a real difference in your life?

My advice: Keep that $5 latte and enjoy every delicious sip. While you're savoring it, brainstorm ways to bring an extra $10,000 in the door.[2]

---

[2] Later in this book, we'll discuss practical ways for you to generate extra money quickly. Keep reading.

"As a Black woman/person of color/queer person/and so on, it is not realistic for me to become wealthy. Society is constructed to make it almost impossible for me to thrive financially. It sucks, it's unfair, but that's just the way it is. Even if I try my absolute hardest, I will never have wealth. It's futile to even try."

This is false. However, it's nuanced. There's truth to this statement, too.

Is our society constructed with racist and oppressive systems that make it difficult for marginalized communities to build wealth? Yes.

But can we create wealth in spite of these very real obstacles? Hell, yes.

Madam C. J. Walker, a Black woman, became America's first female millionaire back in the early 1900s. She started a hair care and beauty business, created her own signature formulas, and trained a fleet of salespeople to get out there and sell these fine products to the masses. She overcame unbelievable challenges. She was ambitious and determined to win. And she made millions.

If she could do it then, more than a hundred years ago, we can absolutely do it now. We have far more advantages today than Walker had back then. She didn't have Google, social media, free online video tutorials, smartphones, or any of the conveniences that we take for granted. She found a way to succeed no matter what, by any means necessary, and we can do the same.

I want to live in a world where million-dollar badasses like Madam C. J. Walker are the norm, not the exception.

To construct that world, there are two kinds of work that need to be done.

There's *community work*—this means dismantling racist, misogynistic, ableist and homophobic systems, getting the right people elected into public office, changing laws, creating new policies that protect systemically marginalized people and ensure we get paid fairly, and ensuring that we don't carry unfair burdens as we march toward wealth.

And, there's *individual work*—this means changing your attitude about money, clearing whatever emotional blocks stand between you and more coin, doing courageous things like starting a business, increasing your prices, negotiating higher pay, and making smart decisions about your finances.

My book, *We Should All Be Millionaires*, and this companion workbook touch upon both types: community work and individual work. However, we primarily focus on individual work because that's the type of work that is 100 percent within your control to do or not do.

You can't always dictate what society chooses to do, but you can take responsibility for your own life. In doing so, you'll inspire others to get onboard and join you.

When enough individual people choose to do the work, it creates a ripple effect, and the community work starts to happen faster, too.

MYTH:

"Becoming a millionaire means exploiting people—such as employees who earn less than I do. I don't want to exploit people. Therefore, I can't become wealthy."

If you don't want to exploit people, it's very simple: *don't*.

Treat your team members with respect, appreciation, and care. Pay them generously. Establish a humane work schedule with space to breathe and rest. Give them ample time off. Create a workplace culture where it is safe for people to be fully themselves.

If you run a company, you can set up a profit-sharing system (as I have). When the company is thriving, every full-time team member gets a hefty bonus check in addition to their regular compensation.

There is more than enough cash to go around. You can build personal wealth for yourself, while helping your team members to thrive financially as well. Do both at the same time.

Over the past few years, numerous people on my team bought homes and new cars, enjoyed paid maternity leave, took family vacations, invested in higher education, and more. I know that I am succeeding as a business owner when my team members have the means to lead a beautiful life.

Becoming wealthy is an opportunity for you to become the best boss imaginable, the kind of employer that people dream of, and wish they could find. You can become the opposite of an exploitative tycoon. Instead of stomping others down in your quest for wealth, you can lift others as you rise.

MYTH:

"I read *We Should All Be Millionaires* and there's some good advice inside . . . for other people. But none of the advice applies to me and my particular situation. It is unrealistic for someone in my line of work to make more money."

A few readers told me something along those lines. Some expressed this in a rather hostile tone (one-star review, I see you!), but I know that is a result of feeling financially frustrated and believing you are permanently stuck.

You may be thinking, *Rachel's advice on how to make more money won't work for me . . .*

"Because I work in an industry where it's not acceptable to charge higher prices."

"Because my clients are low-income and can't afford to pay more than they already do."

"Because I have a regular nine-to-five job. I am not an entrepreneur."

"Because I sell artwork, not professional services like accounting or consulting."

"Because I am a public-school teacher with a fixed salary."

"Because I am a boat captain sailing the high seas and none of your guidance applies to me and my specific industry. You just don't understand maritime life, Rachel! *Ahoy!*"

Okay. Here is the thing. I want to make one point very clear.

No matter who you are—and no matter what you do for a living—you could be earning a lot more money than you currently do.

Read that part again three more times. Let those words sink deeply into your mind. Writing is remembering. Copy that line here and keep it front and center in your memory.

_____

_____

_____

It doesn't matter if you are a visual artist, teacher, lawyer, life coach, activist, or seafaring captain. You could be earning more. Period. There is always a way for you to earn more. The "way" will be slightly different for each person, but there is always a way.

If I were writing a sequel to *We Should All Be Millionaires*, it would probably be called: *Everyone Can Earn More, Yes, Including You, and Yes, I Am Talking to You There, the Very Skeptical Person All the Way in the Back!*

If I suggest something in this workbook that doesn't feel relevant to your exact profession or situation, then, find a way to adapt the suggestion so that it works for you. Pause and ask yourself:

"If this exact thing wouldn't work for me, then, what would work? What's an alternate approach? What's another way to achieve the same goal?"

For instance, you may think to yourself, *I can't launch a business, and I can't take payments from clients/customers, because I don't have a website yet.*

If you don't have a website yet, then, what's another option?

You could install the PayPal or Venmo app on your phone and start taking payments that way. Done.

You may think, *I can't ask my employer for more money because our department is already stretched tight financially.*

If you're unlikely to get a raise this year, what's another option?

You could negotiate for something besides money, like extra time off. Then use your extra time to start a side hustle to increase your income. Eventually that side hustle can become your main hustle.

You may think: *I'm an artist and I sell paintings for $300 each. It takes me several weeks to create each painting. I can't go any faster than I currently do, so I can't earn more.*

If you can't paint faster, what can you do?

You could license your artwork to manufacturers who make throw pillows, wallpaper, and tote bags, so that your art gets featured on items around the world. You could teach a painting class once a month. You could double your prices (and you should). There are probably thirty other things you could do, too.

Even when you feel trapped, you usually are not. There are unlimited possibilities.

You have the ability to earn more money whenever you want to, or need to.

MYTH:

"I don't really 'need' more money. I am doing fine, compared to most.

I don't need more."

Well, I doubt that you picked up this book because money is not that important to you. If this is a common belief you hold, the moral high ground may be keeping your coffers empty. You may think it's noble to claim that money is not that important to you. However, we live in a capitalist society where money is a necessity for survival. It may sound nice to say that you are above making money, but unless you are also above paying rent, eating, and clothing yourself, you're full of shit.

When the women I work with tell me that money is not that important to them, more often than not, they are using their supposed lack of concern about money as a defense mechanism. They know they are capable of making a whole lot more money. On some deep level, they know they are seriously limiting their income and choosing not to live up to their full potential. What they don't know is how to fix it. So they declare "it doesn't matter" to feel better. I get it, I've been there, and I call bullshit. Money isn't everything, but it absolutely is important. Anyone who says it's not is lying.

But let's say you are one of the few women telling the truth when you say that money is not that important to you. Then my next question is: What is important to you? Spending time with family? You need money to go on vacation. Helping others? You can help more people with more money. God? He appreciates donations. Money is not about money, it's about what you are able to do with it.

Now let's get to work.

GOAL: WHAT I WANT YOU TO ACHIEVE

This workbook is a companion to *We Should All Be Millionaires: A Woman's Guide to Earning More, Building Wealth, and Gaining Economic Power.*

I encourage you to read *We Should All Be Millionaires* (or listen to the audiobook) and use this workbook as well. Use both. They go together like peanut butter and jelly. Like Venus and Serena. Like hundred-dollar bills and your wallet.

The Goal of This Workbook

My goal is to:

- Summarize the most important concepts from *We Should All Be Millionaires* in a brief, succinct way, so these concepts stick firmly in your mind. The principle of repetition in education states that learning materials must be repeated many times in order for knowledge to be retained. That is why I have restated some of the core lessons from *We Should All Be Millionaires* in this workbook.

- Shift you from "knowing" to "doing," by giving you powerful action steps that you can take immediately.

- Provide checklists so that you can complete steps, tick things off as you go along, and track your progress.

By the End of This Workbook

After completing this workbook, I expect that you will have:

- A new attitude about money.

- More cash flowing in your bank account.

- More emotional riches, too: hope, peace, power, and joy.

And, by the end of this workbook, I hope you feel like this:

"I am not just 'thinking' about earning more money. I am taking steps to make it happen immediately. Things are in motion!"

"I feel proud of the progress I've made. Maybe I am not a millionaire (yet!), but I am definitely moving in the right direction. I'm on the path to wealth."

"I did a couple things that felt difficult or uncomfortable, and faced some things I've been avoiding. I'm proud of that."

To quote Martin Luther King Jr.:

"Faith is taking the first step even when you don't see the whole staircase."

And, to quote Madam C. J. Walker, Black woman, beauty industry innovator, G.O.A.T., and America's first self-made female millionaire:

"I got my start by giving myself a start."

I hope this workbook can be a powerful start for you.

I know it will be the start of a new chapter in your money story, and the start of a financial future that is so much brighter than your past.

FOR BEST RESULTS, DO THIS

If you are wondering, "How should I use this workbook? How can I get the best results and biggest ROI (return on investment) for the time I put in?"

Here's what I recommend:

1. *Schedule time to do the work, once a week.*

Make a decision right now to commit to this process of taking Million Dollar Action and carve out the time in your calendar to get it done. Get your Google Calendar, day planner, or wherever you keep track of appointments. Schedule a weekly work session. One hour, two hours, whatever you can do.

Call it "Millionaire Work Time" or "Money Date" or "Coins, Coins, Coins" or "Workbook Session" or whatever name you want. Schedule at least ten sessions, one per week, starting this week.

2. *Don't work alone. Do the work with someone else.*

Rather than completing this workbook alone, do the work with someone else—a friend, family member, colleague, coach, or an online community like We Should All Be Millionaires: The Club. (Google it. Join us here: helloseven .co/club. It's incredible.)

Once you've got your money-buddy, read and complete the workbook together.

Or you can do a coworking approach. You can both work on money goals—without necessarily doing the exact same steps.

For instance, on Friday, you can decide, "I'm going to complete one action step from this workbook from 4:00 to 5:00 p.m."

Meanwhile, your coworking friend is going to use that time to write an email to announce that her prices are increasing on January 1. You can both get important things done—at the same time—and keep each other focused.

3. *Every week, give a progress report to someone else.*

Once a week, check with your friend, coach, or coworking buddy and tell that person, "Here's what I said I would accomplish this week. Here's what I actually did. And here's what I plan to do next." Give a status report.

Research from the Association for Talent Development (formerly the American Society of Training & Development) shows that if you do those three things—(1) schedule work time in advance, (2) get an accountability buddy or coach, and (3) give a weekly progress report on how you're doing—you can become 95 percent more likely to succeed with your goal.

If you want maximum ROI, do those three things.

NOTES

MILLION DOLLAR QUESTION

"You can have results or excuses but you can't have both."

—Arnold Schwarzenegger

What are your go-to excuses? You know, the ones you use all the time to get out of taking action.

Write down your top five go-to excuses for not doing the things that you want to be doing. Once you list them here, I want you to take a picture and make it your phone screen or place these five excuses somewhere else you can see them everyday (like your fridge or corkboard), as a reminder that you are so done with excuses and are ready to take action.

1. _____

_____

2. _____

_____

3. _____

_____

4. _____

_____

5. _____

_____

TOPICS AND FORMAT

Here are the topics we're going to cover in this workbook. You'll notice that each topic corresponds to a chapter (with the exact same title) in *We Should All Be Millionaires: A Woman's Guide to Earning More, Building Wealth, and Gaining Economic Power.*

- Million Dollar Story

- Million Dollar Lies

- Million Dollar Decisions

- Million Dollar Boundaries

- Million Dollar Squad

- Million Dollar Vision

- Million Dollar Value

- Million Dollar Pricing

- Million Dollar Team

- Million Dollar Systems

- A Million Dollars Now

Format

For each topic in this workbook (Million Dollar Story, Million Dollar Lies, Million Dollar Decisions, and so on), you will notice the following format:

- Key Points to Know. Quick summary. The main things you need to know about this topic.

- Million Dollar Question. An interesting question to answer. Sometimes, a couple of questions. Write your answer right in the workbook. Or discuss the question with your family, friends, therapist, coach, and other important people in your life. These questions are a great way to spark a conversation about money.

- Million Dollar Action. A money-generating action step for you to do, explained step by step, usually with a worksheet for you to fill out.

- Extra Credit. A little extra for folks who are . . . a little extra. Overachievers out there, I see you.

- Graduation Checklist. Everything you need to do in a tidy list, all in one place. Make sure you've completed all the checklist items before moving to the next section of the workbook. These checklists are a great way to measure your progress. You can see exactly what's done—and what's not done yet.

- Repeat, Repeat, Repeat. You'll see this exact same format repeated in each section: key points, question, action step, extra credit, checklist. Don't you love consistency and repeatable systems? Doesn't that just make you squeal with joy? No? It's just me? Well, okay then.

Enjoy the work. We start now.

MILLION DOLLAR STORY

Your attitude about money was shaped during your childhood and formative years. This story plays out in your head, every day. If this story is helping you, keep it. If it's holding you back, then it's time to pick a new story.

KEY POINTS TO KNOW

Whether you realize it or not, there is a story about money that you routinely tell yourself inside your own head.

This story might sound like, "It's difficult to make money," "I'm good at earning money, but I'm terrible at managing the money I've got," "Artists never earn a good living," or it might be a complicated swirl of several contradictory stories.

It's important to investigate and figure out what kind of money story you are telling yourself. Are you telling yourself a story that's helping you earn more and build wealth? Or a story that's holding you back?

To put it bluntly, are you telling yourself a Broke Ass Story or a Million Dollar Story?

If you're telling yourself a Broke Ass Story, then it will be extremely difficult to create the financial security you want. It's not the only thing holding you back (there are plenty of other things, too, including racism and other systemic issues), but it's one large block in the road. And it's a block that you have the ability to clear out of the way.

Here's the reality: Whenever we tell ourselves stories about the future, we are making things up. We do not know what will happen in the future, therefore any comments or beliefs about what will happen in the future are invented and not real.

If the stories we tell ourselves are made up, why do they matter? Well because the stories we tell ourselves influence the decisions we are making in the present.

For example, if you believe that you will have a successful career, you will make decisions that will usher in that success (for example, investing in additional career training or volunteering to lead meetings). Your belief of the story that your definition of a successful career will definitely happen for you is influencing you to make choices in the present that make that successful career more likely.

Likewise, if you believe that you will die young, you may think it really doesn't matter if you take care of your health. You might do nothing to stop the series of unhealthy daily habits you have, making it more likely that you will die young.

If we are all just inventing stories anyway, why not choose to believe positive stories that give you hope and have a positive impact on your life? Instead of telling yourself stories that make you feel dejected and helpless.

When you change the story you are telling yourself about money, you will make financial decisions that serve you well, and you will feel more confident while you do it.

NOTES

MILLION DOLLAR QUESTIONS

What is one thought about money that you have on a regular basis? Something that you think to yourself pretty often—several times a week, perhaps daily. Write it down.

_____

_____

_____

_____

If you had to guess, where do you think this particular thought came from? Did you absorb this way of thinking from your family, friends, mentors, society as a whole, or somewhere else?

_____

_____

_____

_____

_____

Do you feel this particular thought is helping you or holding you back?

_____

_____

_____

_____

_____

MILLION DOLLAR ACTION

Learn how to think like a millionaire. Upgrade your thoughts.

Read through the following list of Broke Ass Stories v. Million Dollar Stories. At the end of the chart, write down several Broke Ass Stories that you think on a regular basis. Next to each one, write a Million Dollar Story that you can start thinking instead.

BROKE ASS STORIES	MILLION DOLLAR STORIES
The world is unfair, so I am not going to bother trying.	The world is unfair, and I'm going to be a millionaire to make the world a better place.
I'll never get out of debt.	I am capable of changing my situation.
Making money is hard.	There are infinite ways to make money. I can find something that feels good to me. It may be challenging but also fun and worthwhile.
Making money is too risky.	I am scrappy as hell, and I will always land on my feet.
I'm not good with money.	Building wealth is a skill that I can learn.
I'll always be broke.	The past has passed, the future is rich. My future can be different from my past.
Rich people are assholes.	Poor and rich people can be assholes, and poor and rich people can be kind. If I'm an asshole, it's not money's fault.
People won't like me if I have money.	There are seven billion people living on planet Earth. It is not possible to be liked by all seven billion. Striving to be universally liked is a game I can't win. My true friends will love me regardless of my income level.

BROKE ASS STORIES	MILLION DOLLAR STORIES
Money changes people.	Yeah, money absolutely changes your life. Now you have a house, a car, and all your needs met without ever having to worry about bills. Holla!
If I get rich, people will only want me for my money.	I can find dope friends who celebrate my success at every income level.
Making more money is gonna make my life more complicated. In other words, mo' money, mo' problems.	Money doesn't solve every problem, but it can solve a lot of them. Let it be easy.
I don't know what I would do with more money.	I trust myself to use my money to do great things for myself and others.
I'm too tired to make more money.	Making money is energizing.
I'm not smart, creative, genius, or entrepreneurial enough to make a lot of money.	There are plenty of stupid people who are super rich, surely I am smarter than those people.
Whenever I get money, I always screw it up.	I've made Broke Ass Decisions (a.k.a. BADs) in the past, but now I'm making Million Dollar Decisions (a.k.a. MDDs).
I'll never get out of this hole. I accept defeat.	It might take me a while to reach my goals or it might not, but either way, it's more fun to try. Many people have hit rock bottom and then have gone on to create amazing things. I can be one of them. My story isn't over yet.

BROKE ASS STORIES	MILLION DOLLAR STORIES

BROKE ASS STORIES	MILLION DOLLAR STORIES

EXTRA CREDIT

Now that you have reframed those Broke Ass Stories into Million Dollar Stories, I'd like you to solidify these new stories in your brain with evidence.

Choose one of your top three Broke Ass Stories (the ones you believed the most). Write down the new Million Dollar Story you are choosing to believe instead. Then create a list of three pieces of evidence from the past or present that prove that this new Million Dollar Story is actually true.

Here's an example:

Broke Ass Story: I'll never get out of debt.

Million Dollar Story: I am capable of changing my situation.

Evidence #1: Madam CJ Walker is an example of a person who was destitute and yet she found a way to become a millionaire. If she can do it in the early 1900s, surely I can do it now.

Evidence #2: When I was in college, I owed $5,000 on a credit card and I thought I would never pay it off. But shortly after graduating from college and getting my first full-time job, I was able to pay off that credit card. I've gotten out of debt before so I can do it again.

Evidence #3: I know entrepreneurs that have built successful businesses generating over $100k in revenue in just a year or less. If they can earn an extra $100k in less than a year, it's possible that I can too.

Broke Ass Story #1: _____

_____

_____

Million Dollar Story: _____

_____

_____

Evidence #1: _____

_____

_____

Evidence #2: _____

_____

_____

Evidence #3: _____

_____

_____

Broke Ass Story #2: _____

_____

_____

Million Dollar Story: _____

_____

_____

Evidence #1: _____

_____

_____

Evidence #2: _____

_____

_____

Evidence #3: _____

_____

_____

Broke Ass Story #3: _____

_____

_____

Million Dollar Story: _____

_____

_____

Evidence #1: _____

_____

_____

Evidence #2: _____

_____

_____

Evidence #3: _____

_____

_____

GRADUATION CHECKLIST

To graduate from this section—"Million Dollar Stories"—and move along to the next section of the workbook, complete the following items.
Be sure to check off every item before moving to the next section.

☐ Answer the Million Dollar Questions on page 31 of this workbook.

☐ Read through the list of Broke Ass Stories v. Million Dollar Stories on pages 32–33 of this workbook.

☐ Choose a few Broke Ass Stories that you have on a fairly regular basis. Next to each one, write a Million Dollar Story that you can choose to think instead. You can do this on pages 34–35.

☐ Extra credit: Prove that your Million Dollar Stories are true by writing down three pieces of evidence that help you to believe your top three Million Dollar Stories (instead of your Broke Ass Stories).

☐ Highly recommended: Open the book *We Should All Be Millionaires*. Read the chapter "Million Dollar Stories" to go even deeper into this topic.

☐ Fill in the blank: "The main thing I learned from this section is

_____

_____

_____

_____

_____

_____"

☐ All done? Excellent! Celebrate your progress with a frothy latte or glass of rosé, then sashay along to the next section.

MILLION
DOLLAR LIES

*T*he media and our government have reinforced messages that women are bad with money. This is a lie. It's time to separate the lies from the truth, forgive yourself, and heal your relationship with money.

KEY POINTS TO KNOW

Open any glossy magazine or watch any TV sitcom. As women, we are constantly inundated with messages from the media that we are shopaholics buying way too many shoes, maxing out credit cards, and making poor financial decisions.

When you are told something over and over, practically beaten over the head with it, eventually, it starts to feel like the truth.

For centuries, the government has reinforced these messages with laws designed to choke women's earning potential. Laws to prevent women from owning property, getting a college degree, starting a business, or even something as basic as opening a bank account in her own name.

Many of these oppressive laws have changed in the last hundred years or so (weak applause, side-eye, hooray?). But these legal changes are more recent than you might think.

For instance, until 1974, women couldn't do things like purchase a car or get a credit card without the approval and cosign of a man, such as her father or husband.

Men have had a two-hundred-year head start[3] on building wealth here in the United States and in many parts around the world. Women have only had fifty years, and already we have women millionaires, billionaires, and presidential candidates. It goes to show how powerful we are, how much we've

[3] At least! More like a two-thousand-year head start, really.

achieved in so little time, in spite of the many ways that our government has been complicit in holding us back.

Point being, there are many reasons why you, as a woman, struggle to earn more and build wealth.

Some of these reasons are blocks you've created yourself—a financial prison of your own making. But many other reasons are systemic, historic, existed long before you were born, and are not your fault. Like a fish swimming in a poisoned tank, you didn't put the poison there yourself. Someone else did. But you suffer the consequences nonetheless.

When it comes to your financial situation, it's important to take responsibility for the parts that you can control and improve. When you take responsibility, you also take power.

And, it's equally important to *shed* responsibility for the parts that are not your fault.

Forgive yourself for mistakes you've made in the past and stop berating yourself for struggling with money. Instead of blaming yourself, place the blame where it is rightfully due. Instead of being cruel to yourself, speak to yourself like a friend and make moves that improve your prospects.

NOTES

MILLION DOLLAR QUESTIONS

What is one lie about money that you've been told repeatedly by the media, government, society, and so on?

This might be something like, "A salary of $100,000 per year is plenty of money for a family of four living in San Francisco," "Banks treat everyone fairly," "Women are bad with money," or "The gender pay gap doesn't exist."

When it comes to your current financial situation, describe something for which you claim full responsibility? And describe something that is *not* your fault? It is important to know the difference.

Fill in the blanks: "I take full responsibility for _____. However, _____ is not my fault."

Do a Financial Forgiveness Ritual.

Get a pen. Light a candle. Settle in. Take your time with this exercise. Make a list of every financial mistake you feel you've made in the past. Big things. Small things. All the things. Write it all down.

For example:

"I forgive myself for . . . allowing my narcissistic ex-boyfriend to live at my apartment rent-free for six months even though he was perfectly capable of contributing."

"I forgive myself for . . . undercharging for so many years because I was afraid to ask for more."

"I forgive myself for . . . allowing myself to get distracted by petty, trivial, piddly nonsense instead of focusing on making money. I wasted a lot of time and I forgive myself for that."

And so on.

You might write down three things that you want to forgive and release them. You might write down a hundred things. Keep writing until you feel "done," like you've truly emptied it all out. Use a notebook if you need more space to write.

I forgive myself for . . .

_____

_____

_____

_____

_____

_____

_____

_____

_____

_____

Once you're done writing, do something to symbolize releasing all the heaviness from your life.

You can tear out a page from this workbook, crumple up the paper, and burn it.

You can fold the paper into a beautiful origami shape to represent your transformation, turning the pain of the past into something new and beautiful.

You can set this workbook aside and go take a hot shower or jump into a cold river. Wash the past away. Or scream it out, shake it out, dance it out, whatever you feel called to do. Do something that feels cleansing and cathartic.

You don't need to carry this heaviness any longer. All the shame, guilt, anger, and resentment that have built up in the past—they are not helping you reach your financial goals. They're just weighing you down and making the journey slower than it needs to be. Choose to let it go and move on. Forgiveness is a gift to yourself.

EXTRA CREDIT

Choose one especially painful mistake. Find gratitude for it.

You have probably learned priceless lessons as a result of hurt, pain, or struggle.

Choose one financial mistake from the past that feels especially painful. Then, find one reason to feel grateful that this happened. Reframe the situation in a new light.

Perhaps you feel grateful because you learned what *not* to do again, or how *not* to be a boss, or how *not* to do your taxes.

Write down what you learned.

Fill in the blanks: "Even though _____

_____

_____

was really painful, I can find gratitude that it happened because it taught me

_____

_____

_____."

GRADUATION CHECKLIST

To graduate from this section—"Million Dollar Lies"—and move along to the next section of the workbook, complete the following items.

Be sure to check off every item before moving to the next section.

- ☐ Answer the Million Dollar Questions on page 45 of this workbook.

- ☐ Do the Financial Forgiveness Ritual described on page 46 of this workbook.

- ☐ Extra credit: Choose one financial mistake from the past that feels especially painful. Find gratitude for it. Identify something you learned from that experience.

- ☐ Highly recommended: Open the book *We Should All Be Millionaires*. Read the chapter "Million Dollar Lies" to go even deeper into this topic.

- ☐ Fill in the blank, "I used to believe _____

_____

_____, but I recognize now, this is a lie."

MILLION DOLLAR
DECISIONS

The road to riches is paved with Million Dollar Decisions. If you want to be wealthy, you have to start making Million Dollar Decisions instead of Broke Ass Decisions.

Million Dollar Decisions:

- Create time and energy

- Free up mental space

- Reduce piddly nonsense

- Make you feel strong, secure, and free

- Create options instead of eliminating options

- Bring you more wealth: financial wealth, emotional wealth, usually both

Broke Ass Decisions (BADs) have the opposite effect. They:

- Steal your time and energy

- Deplete your mental space

- Increase piddly crap and leave little room for your greatest desires

- Make you feel weak, insecure, and trapped

- Eliminate options rather than creating them

- Drain your bank account or hinder you from earning more

A few examples follow:

Broke Ass Decision

Letting house guests stay with you for a week, even though you know they will disrupt your work, peace, and well-being.

Million Dollar Decision

Telling your guests they can stay with you for two nights and giving them a list of hotels where they can stay for the remainder of their trip.

Broke Ass Decision

Your car broke down and you take it to the mechanic to fix for the third time this year.

Million Dollar Decision

You head to the dealer and trade in your broken-down car for a reliable, certified, pre-owned car because time is money.

Broke Ass Decision

You don't want to hire help in your business (or you're afraid to do it), so you spend twenty hours per week doing tedious, time-sucking administrative work that you really have no business doing.

Million Dollar Decision

You recognize the value of your work, so you hire a part-time assistant for twenty hours per week, and you spend your freed-up time acquiring more clients and making more money.

Why do so many women make Broke Ass Decisions?

The top reasons women tend to make BADs are her desire to be liked (doesn't want to ruffle feathers or rock the boat), the influence of Broke Ass Decisionmakers (hanging with the wrong people who bring you down), and living in a Broke Ass Environment (cluttered, unpleasant space that drains your energy).

Continue making BADs and you will stay broke.

Start making MDDs and your life will change rapidly.

Not sure how to make Million Dollar Decisions? We made a handy formula for you, which you'll learn in just a moment. Use this formula to evaluate any situation, weigh your options, and make better decisions. Begin with the very next decision you make.

NOTES

MILLION DOLLAR QUESTIONS

Write down three Broke Ass Decisions that you made in the last year or so.

This could be things like "undercharging for my services," "allowing my cousin to move into my spare room, indefinitely, rent-free," "giving too much to others while neglecting my health," or anything else. (Vow: never again!)

_____

_____

_____

_____

_____

Write down three Million Dollar Decisions that you made in the last year or so.

This could be things like, "raising my prices," "investing in new clothes that help me feel confident during meetings at work," "getting a healthy meal delivery service," or "launching my side hustle and getting my first paying client!" Celebrate these wins!

_____

_____

_____

_____

_____

_____

MILLION DOLLAR ACTION

Learn the We Should All Be Millionaires (WSABM) formula for making better decisions. Use this formula to make one decision, right now.

It is challenging to make Million Dollar Decisions in a world that constantly tells you that you are only worthy of brokenness. So, we created a formula (and initialism) to help you evaluate options and make better decisions.

The initialism goes:

W is for Want. What do you really *want* to do?
S is for Should. What do you feel you *should* do?
A is for Action. What *action* will you take to get what you want?
B is for Body. How does your *body* feel about taking that action?
M is for More. What will you have *more* of if you make this decision?

Practice right now.
What's a decision you need to make?
Maybe you need to make a decision about your career, schedule, pricing, boundaries, a project you're considering, an investment you might make, or something else. Evaluate your options using the WSABM formula.

W is for Want.
What do I want to do?
What do I want to prioritize?
[If you're considering several different options/possibilities] If any of these options could be the right decision, which one do I want it to be?

_____

_____

_____

_____

_____

_____

S is for Should.

What "shoulds" are present?

What is my brain telling me I "should" do, and is that actually true? Or is it just fear, self-doubt, or the patriarchy barking at me?

_____

_____

_____

_____

_____

_____

_____

_____

_____

_____

A is for Action.

What course of action will I take to move toward what I want?

What are the first small steps I will take?

_____

_____

_____

_____

_____

_____

_____

_____

_____

B is for Body.

[Close your eyes and imagine taking this course of action.]

As I see myself doing what I want, how does my body feel? Relaxed, joyful, expanding? What feelings arise?

_____

_____

_____

_____

_____

_____

_____

_____

M is for More.

How will this course of action generate "more" in my life?

Will it bring me more money, more emotional wealth, more time, energy, peace, power, joy?

What will I get more of in my life, my relationships, my work, my personal growth?

_____

_____

_____

_____

_____

_____

_____

Make Your Decision

After going through the WSABM formula, make your decision.

My situation is . . .

_____

_____

_____

_____

_____

_____

_____

_____

_____

_____

I am considering a few options, including . . .

_____

_____

_____

_____

_____

_____

_____

_____

_____

_____

_____

After doing the WSABM formula, I realize that . . .

_____

_____

_____ would be a Broke Ass Decision.

_____

_____

_____ feels like a Million Dollar Decision.

So, I'm going to do that.

EXTRA CREDIT

Do an environmental detox (a.k.a.: clean up your Broke Ass Environment)

Look around. Notice what's in your environment. Assess your physical surroundings, your home, your wardrobe, your possessions. Consider the media messages you are taking in, the news you read, the shows you watch, what you put on your calendar, because these are part of your environment, too.

What do you see?

Perhaps, a cluttered shelf. Clothes that don't fit. Mildew on the shower curtain. A schedule crammed with things you hate doing. Everything in your environment hugely impacts how you feel.

Notice whether your environment is sending you messages of abundance or messages like "never enough," "shabbiness," "financial anxiety," "existential anxiety," "settling or making do," or "do more with less."

Do an environmental detox to clear these Broke Ass Signals out of your space.

Write down five things that you're willing to declutter/eliminate from your environment. This could be physical items (clothes, furniture, junk mail, and so on), schedule-clutter, brain-clutter, any kind of dreary clutter. Get these out of your space. You will feel better immediately.

1. _____

   _____

   _____

2. _____

   _____

   _____

3. _____

   _____

   _____

4. _____

   _____

   _____

5. _____

   _____

   _____

GRADUATION CHECKLIST

To graduate from this section—"Million Dollar Decisions"—and move along to the next section of the workbook, complete the following items. Be sure to check off every item before moving to the next section.

- ☐ Answer the Million Dollar Questions on page 56 of this workbook.

- ☐ Learn the We Should All Be Millionaires (WSABM) formula for making better decisions, described on page 57 of this workbook. Use this formula to make one decision right now.

- [ ] Clap your hands emphatically and declare to yourself, your dog, your houseplant, or whoever is nearby: *No. More. Broke. Ass. Decisions.*

- [ ] Extra credit: Do an environmental detox, as described on page 61.

- [ ] Highly recommended: Open the book *We Should All Be Millionaires*. Read the chapter "Million Dollar Decisions" to go even deeper into this topic.

- [ ] Fill in the blank, "The very next Million Dollar Decision I'm going to make is _____

_____

_____

_____."

MILLION DOLLAR BOUNDARIES

*W*omen have historically been responsible for the majority of housework while getting the short end of the stick in the workplace. You need to stop over-giving and create clear boundaries to protect your time, energy, and money.

KEY POINTS TO KNOW

It's nice to think that men and women share household labor equally (after all, this isn't 1950 anymore), but sadly this is not the case.

Even today, in our supposedly advanced and progressive society, women still do the majority of both visible and invisible domestic labor (laundry, cooking, cleaning, caregiving, nurturing, remembering when Shonda's next dental cleaning appointment is happening, and so on).

Even in two-parent households where both parents have full-time careers, women tend to do significantly more housework and unpaid labor than her male partner.

One harrowing example: Most women spend more than two hundred hours per year washing and folding laundry. Imagine reclaiming those two hundred hours and using that time to launch a business, find more clients, and increase your income. Or using that time to relax and enjoy your damn life!

Women also get the short end of the stick in the workplace, causing our labor not to be properly remunerated and respected.

At work, we over-give and under-earn. At home, we start our "second shift" and work even more while our housemates relax on the couch in blissful ignorance (or help out but do the absolute bare minimum).

Instead of mapping out seven-figure business plans, we spend an eternity folding undies.

This must change. The solution is to set boundaries to protect your time, space, mental energy, and other resources. Once communicated, boundaries must be enforced to properly serve their purpose. A boundary is worthless unless you actually enforce it.

Setting a boundary doesn't mean "bossing other people around." It's really not about other people at all. It's about you.

Setting a boundary means that you refuse to tolerate a crappy situation any longer, and you are raising the standard for how your life functions. It's giving yourself an upgrade to something better, instead of continuing to settle for crumbs.

MILLION DOLLAR QUESTIONS

What areas of your life are exhausting, crappy, not okay, in urgent need of an upgrade?

Write down five things you are sick and tired of doing. Or write down five areas in your life where you have been settling for crumbs.

1. _____

    Upgrade: _____

2. _____

    Upgrade: _____

3. _____

    Upgrade: _____

4. _____

    Upgrade: _____

5. _____

    Upgrade: _____

Under each item you wrote down, write a beautiful upgrade—something that would immediately improve the situation. A new, higher standard of living.

For instance, instead of spending two hundred hours a year doing laundry, you could hire a pick-up and drop-off service to do it. Instead of answering client emails on weekends, you could S-T-O-P. And so on. By writing "better options" and "upgrades," you're discovering new boundaries that you need to set and enforce.

MILLION DOLLAR ACTION

Choose one thing you are done tolerating, set a boundary, and then communicate that boundary to whoever needs to know.

I am so done with . . .

_____

_____

_____

_____

_____

_____

_____

_____

_____

From now on, my new boundary is . . .

_____

_____

_____

_____

_____

_____

_____

_____

_____

_____

In order to set up this boundary and make it happen, I need to . . .

I need to notify the following people about this new boundary . . .

If someone forgets about this boundary, pushes back, or tries to violate it, I will . . .

_____

_____

_____

_____

_____

_____

EXTRA CREDIT

Calculate the cost of weak, nonexistent boundaries.

Think about an area of your life where you need boundaries.

Now, imagine that you decide *not* to change anything. You let things continue as is. You continue to do the majority of the household labor. You continue to over-deliver and undercharge. You continue to let friends and family members use you as their personal maid, chauffeur, concierge service, and therapist.

Consider, "What is the cost if I allow this to continue?"

What is the price you pay? What will you lose? Take a guess. Time, energy, sleep, health, years of your life, opportunities, joy, peace, mental health, millions of dollars, something else?

_____

_____

_____

_____

_____

_____

Confronting the cost can be startling. This might be exactly what you need to see to get motivated and set boundaries.

GRADUATION CHECKLIST

To graduate from this section—"Million Dollar Boundaries"—and move along to the next section of the workbook, complete the following items. Be sure to check off every item before moving to the next section.

- ☐ Answer the Million Dollar Questions on page 69 of this workbook.

- ☐ Choose one thing you are done tolerating, set a new boundary, and then communicate that boundary to whoever needs to know. Nail down your plan for this on page 70.

- ☐ Extra credit: Calculate the cost of weak or nonexistent boundaries in your life. Write down the price you will pay if you allow this to continue. Do this on page 72.

- ☐ Highly recommended: Open the book *We Should All Be Millionaires*. Read the chapter "Million Dollar Boundaries" to go even deeper into this topic.

- ☐ Fill in the blanks: "I am done settling for _____

_____

_____.

From now on, I require _____

_____

_____."

MILLION
DOLLAR SQUAD

*N*inety-five percent of your success can be predicted by the people with whom you regularly spend time. You need to create a strong support network in order to make millions. And, no, you don't need a white male mentor to invite you to have a seat at the table. You can build your own table.

KEY POINTS TO KNOW

To become a wealthy, successful, high-achieving person, you need a rock-solid support squad.

You need trusted advisors. You need close friends with whom you can vent in tough moments, people who will keep your secrets with the utmost confidentiality. You need people who will check on you to make sure you're progressing with your goals (#accountability).

If you surround yourself with ambitious, successful women who are making big money, the golden-money-dust rubs off on you. You become more successful, too.

Unfortunately, many women lack a powerful network, and this contributes to the gender and racial pay gaps and continued inequality when it comes to access to opportunity.

Women are often taught that having white male allies is essential to our success. This is bullshit. Research shows that white men gonna help white men. Don't look for a man to be your savior or open doors for you because most likely it ain't gonna happen. Women should seek to create an inner circle of close women friends.

Even if you're shy, introverted, or live in a remote location without access to city amenities, you can create your Million Dollar Squad.

Your Million Dollar Squad should include people who . . .

- Bring wealth, energy, power, peace, and/or joy into your life consistently.

- Bring financial riches into your life (client referrals, job leads, genius moneymaking ideas).

- Bring emotional riches into your life (boost your mood, make you believe you can do anything, inspire you to take better care of yourself, make you laugh like a hyena).

- Help you climb that Million Dollar Mountain like a trusted mountain-climbing guide, moving you closer and closer to the peak.

- Give and receive mutual support and respect—in other words, you add something magical to these people's lives, and elevate them, too.

There are plenty of ways to build a Million Dollar Squad.

You can join an online community, network, or club and find like-minded people there. You can attend a workshop, and your new bestie might be seated right next to you nibbling a cinnamon bun (this happened to me!). You can reach out to people you already know and deepen those relationships. You can start a podcast, interview fascinating people, and many of those folks might become your friends (also me). There are many ways to do it. Pick something and get on it.

Bottom line: You need to surround yourself with people who've got a Million Dollar Attitude—people who inspire you to be your best.

Do this, and your financial situation will change. Don't do this, and you'll struggle to earn more and build wealth.

MILLION DOLLAR QUESTIONS

Who are three people who inspire you to be your best?

Who are three people who deplete you, distract you, or make it difficult for you to stay focused on your money goals? (Perhaps it's time to do a friend audit and eliminate these relationships. Or, at least, distance yourself.)

What do you bring to the table? As a friend, what do you offer to the people in your life? Why would people want you in their squad? Write down some of your best attributes, qualities, and assets.

Build Your Million Dollar Squad

What kind of support do you need? What kind of people can give you that support? Create a specific plan and start building your squad.

I need support with . . .

- Working through my limiting beliefs around money.

- Figuring out how to make way more money without burning out.

- Balancing my passion for my business with my mental health.

- Something else.

I can get that support from . . .

- A life or business coach who has similar life experiences to mine.

- A community of entrepreneurs of color.

- A therapist who specializes in supporting Black women.

- Something else.

_____

_____

_____

_____

_____

_____

_____

_____

_____

_____

_____

_____

If I was building a Million Dollar Squad with seven incredible people in it, my dream squad would include . . .

_____

_____

_____

EXTRA CREDIT

Reconnect with the community you already have.

Most likely, you already know some incredible people. But maybe you've allowed these relationships to wither. It happens. Reconnect and recommit to building those relationships.

Reach out to rekindle the relationship. It doesn't take much. One act of kindness or generosity can go a very long way.

Rather than just reaching out to say, "Hey, thinking of you," reach out to say, "I mentioned you on my podcast," "I nominated you for an award," "I referred a client to you, hope that's cool," "I popped something in the mail for you."

Be generous and create miracles for people, and they'll become loyal friends for life.

Write a list of people who inspire you, but with whom you haven't connected in a while. For each person, come up with something you could do for (or with) them. For example:

Giselle: Send a free sample of my handmade soap in the mail and send a text to let her know a surprise is on the way.

Nico: Invite for a brunch and biz talk.

Martina: Refer a client to her, and email to let her know.

1. _____

_____

_____

_____

2. _____

_____

_____

_____

3. _____

_____

_____

_____

4. _____

_____

_____

_____

5. _____

_____

_____

_____

GRADUATION CHECKLIST

To graduate from this section—"Million Dollar Squad"—and move along to the next section of the workbook, complete the following items.

Be sure to check off every item before moving to the next section.

☐ Answer the Million Dollar Questions on page 79 of this workbook.

☐ Create a plan to build your Million Dollar Squad. Write down what kind of support you need right now, and where you're gonna get it. Do this on page 80.

☐ Extra credit: Reach out to someone you already know, someone who inspires you, but with whom you haven't connected in a while. Do something generous to surprise this person and rekindle the relationship.

☐ Highly recommended: Open the book *We Should All Be Millionaires*. Read the chapter called "Million Dollar Squad" to go even deeper into this topic.

☐ Fill in the blanks: "One relationship that I want to deepen is with

_____

_____

_____

_____.

One relationship that I want to distance myself from (or eliminate completely) is with _____

_____

_____

_____."

MILLION
DOLLAR VISION

*B*e extravagant with your dreams and goals. Create a Million Dollar Vision for your life—a vision that is beautiful, ambitious, and worth getting excited about. Shift your language to lean into possibility rather than defeat.

KEY POINTS TO KNOW

You want to have more money and have a rich and abundant life. But what does "having more" look like for you?

Do you want a four-bedroom house in the hippest area of town, or a remote cottage in the woods? Do you want a nanny, chef, personal trainer, or all the above? Want to buy an apartment for your mom so that she can enjoy her retirement years without stress? Leave behind a sizable legacy for your kids?

What does "live like a millionaire" mean to you?

It's important to create a clear vision of what you want. Because you can't hit the target if you don't even know what the target is.

Give yourself permission to dream big and create a Million Dollar Vision for your life—a vision of exactly what you want, down to the smallest detail, like the zip code for your new home, and the make and model of the car you desire. Be extravagant with your desires and be specific.

It may take five years to make this Million Dollar Vision a reality. It may take three years. Or one year.

As you work toward this vision, you are becoming a new woman—a millionaire version of yourself. You can behave like that woman right now. Set goals like her. Set boundaries like her. Be Her Now.

Even if you're currently earning very little, you can start behaving like the most successful, wealthy version of yourself. Be Her Now, and you will *actually* become her much faster.

Being Her Now is not about spending money. It's about how you treat yourself and spend your time. You don't need to accumulate debt or buy thousand-dollar designer heels to start behaving like a woman who makes millions.

Last, watch the way you talk about your goals and dreams. Shift your language to lean toward possibility rather than defeat.

If you notice yourself using doubtful, hesitant language like, "If my plan works out," "Maybe, assuming things go according to plan," "I'll need to wait and see," "I'm not sure that's realistic right now," "I probably need a backup plan," catch yourself and adjust your language.

Speak words of conviction and power.

"I expect," not "I hope." "I will," not "I might." "I know," not "I'm not sure." "When I'm a millionaire," not "If I become a millionaire."

Plan to win instead of planning to fail. Speak like someone who expects to succeed.

NOTES

MILLION DOLLAR QUESTION

Imagine the most successful, affluent version of yourself—a woman whose bank account is full, whose dreams are fully realized, who feels secure and powerful.

How could you Be Her Now?

What are some things you could do to feel like her, behave like her, live like her, even if you're not earning seven figures per year, at least not yet?

For example, perhaps you could:

- Invest in one bottle of perfume that you really love.

- Create a wellness plan and commit to it. Daily walks. Daily workouts (gentle movement totally counts). Fresh air. Nature.

- Do something every morning that makes you feel "pulled together" and "bossed up," whatever that means for you. Mascara. A cute silk scarf. Meditation. Whatevs.

- Write down at least five ideas to Be Her Now.

1. _____

2. _____

3. _____

4. _____

5. _____

MILLION DOLLAR ACTION

Make a list of everything you want—your absolute dream life. Then, do the math. Figure out how much your dream life would actually cost.

What is your Million Dollar Vision—your dream life, a life where you have everything you could possibly want and feel like a million bucks?

How much would your dream life actually cost? Would it cost $5,000 per month, $10,000, $35,000, or what?

It's time to crunch the numbers and figure it out.

Below, next to each category (home, transportation, wardrobe, and so on), write down your dream situation. Write down what you really want, not what you think you can currently afford.

You want a four-bedroom home in the country with a pool? You want a new Lexus with all the latest safety features? You fantasize about having a personal chef who handles dinners on weeknights? Write it down.

Home / Physical Space

_____

_____

_____

_____

_____

_____

_____

_____

_____

_____

_____

Transportation

Wardrobe

Self-Care / Daily Habits

_____

_____

_____

_____

_____

_____

_____

_____

_____

_____

Household Work / Hired Help

_____

_____

_____

_____

_____

_____

_____

_____

_____

_____

_____

_____

Recreation / Travel

Education (Self and Kids)

Savings / Investments

_____
_____
_____
_____
_____
_____
_____
_____
_____
_____

Giving / Community Contributions

_____
_____
_____
_____
_____
_____
_____
_____
_____
_____
_____

Other Things I Want

_____

_____

_____

_____

_____

_____

_____

_____

_____

_____

Once you've written down everything that your dream life would include, then start researching. Get thee to Google! Find out how much each thing would actually cost.

You can research online and find the cost for literally anything. Type into the search field, "How much is a four-bedroom house near Lake Norman in North Carolina" or "How much is a personal chef in Chicago" or "How much is a private SAT tutor in New York City" and, bingo, you will have the numbers.

Get a number for each item in your vision. It's okay if it's not exact. A rough estimate is fine. Add it all up to figure out, "This is how much it would cost to live my dream life."

The cost might be more than you think. It might be less. You won't know until you do the math.

This is a powerful step, because you're getting clear on what you actually want, and what it would actually cost.

Instead of vaguely saying, "I want to have more money" or "I want to live differently," now, you have a Million Dollar Vision that is specific.

Home / Physical Space

_____

_____

Total Monthly Cost: _____

Transportation

_____

_____

Total Monthly Cost: _____

Wardrobe

_____

_____

Total Monthly Cost: _____

Self-Care / Daily Habits

_____

_____

Total Monthly Cost: _____

Household Work / Hired Help

_____

_____

Total Monthly Cost: _____

Recreation / Travel

_____

_____

Total Monthly Cost: _____

Education (Self and Kids)

_____

_____

Total Monthly Cost: _____

Savings / Investments

_____

_____

Total Monthly Cost: _____

Giving / Community Contributions

_____

_____

Total Monthly Cost: _____

Other Things I Want

_____

_____

Total Monthly Cost: _____

My Million Dollar Vision (a.k.a. my dream life) costs approximately
_____ per month.

EXTRA CREDIT

Brainstorm twenty-five moneymaking ideas

You wrote down everything your dream life would include. You did the math to figure out how much it would cost.

Let's say that your dream life (a.k.a. your Million Dollar Vision) costs $28,000 per month. Cool. This is your new monthly income target. Maybe you currently earn $9,000 per month, which means you want to earn $19,000 more.

Brainstorm a list of twenty-five ways that you could bring that additional money in the door. Write down any and all ideas, no matter how wacky they seem.

Could you start a side hustle teaching workshops on weekends? Could you get hired for a lucrative speaking engagement? Could you write a book that sells a thousand copies per month? Could you train people to do whatever you do (nails, legal services, dog walking) to expand your team and scale your income, too? And what else?

1. _____

2. _____

3. _____

4. _____

5. _____

6. _____

7. _____

8. _____

9. _____

10. _____

11. _____

12. _____

13. _____

14. _____

15. _____

16. _____

17. _____

18. _____

19. _____

20. _____

21. _____

22. _____

24. _____

25. _____

You don't need to do everything on your list. In fact, you probably shouldn't. But out of those twenty-five ideas, one or two might be Million Dollar Ideas.

The goal here is to crack open your mind, start thinking in new ways, and remind yourself: "There are so many ways to bring more money in the door. I have many options. My Million Dollar Vision is attainable."

GRADUATION CHECKLIST

To graduate from this section—"Million Dollar Vision"—and move along to the next section of the workbook, complete the following items.

Be sure to check off every item before moving to the next section.

☐ Answer the Million Dollar Question on page 89 of this workbook.

☐ Make a list of everything you want—your absolute dream life, your Million Dollar Vision. Then, do the math. Figure out how much your dream life would actually cost. Add it up to find your new monthly income target. Do this on page 90.

☐ Extra credit: Brainstorm a list of twenty-five ways that you could bring more money in the door. You can write down ideas on page 98.

☐ Highly recommended: Open the book *We Should All Be Millionaires*. Read the chapter "Million Dollar Vision" to go even deeper into this topic.

☐ Fill in the blank, "I may not be a millionaire (yet), but I can start behaving like a wealthy woman right now. One way that I can Be Her Now is _____

_____   _____

_____."

You've reached the middle of this workbook.

Take a moment to pause. Celebrate all the work you've completed so far.

Whatever stage of the millionaire journey you're at, each stage is exciting in its own way.

If you have zero money in your bank account, that means you have a blank slate, you can start your journey on a strong note, and literally anything is possible.

If you have millions in the bank, that means you have considerable economic power and abundant options in life.

If you're somewhere in between, that means there are victories to celebrate and more work to be done.

If you're at the top, enjoy the view.

If you're at the bottom, enjoy the climb.

Take a moment to write down some of your favorite insights you've had while working through this workbook.

Key Insights Thus Far:

_____

_____

_____

_____

_____

_____

_____

MILLION DOLLAR VALUE

What is something you can do that is extremely valuable? Identify what makes you valuable, believe it, own it, and charge accordingly.

KEY POINTS TO KNOW

You need to spend some time thinking about the question:

"What could I offer to the world that is extremely valuable?"

This is *the* Million Dollar Question.

The answer might be staring you right in the face. It might be something you already do in your current career (and you just need to start charging a whole lot more). It could be something you do just for fun in your spare time (that you could start charging for). It could be something that comes naturally to you, so naturally you never even recognized that this is a valuable gift.

Once you identify the valuable talent that you have, believe it, own it, and charge accordingly. Your life will change forever.

The tricky snag is that you may not "see" just how valuable you are, even if others can see it plain as day.

You may have a nasty case of imposter syndrome. You probably have been overworking and undercharging for your entire life. In fact, I would bet you're undercharging so severely that you could double your rates and your work would *still* be an absolute bargain.

Not understanding your value and not charging what you're worth are literally costing you millions. You're leaving money on the table due to self-doubt and lack of clarity. Now is the moment to get clear on the value you provide.

MILLION DOLLAR QUESTIONS

What are the things that come naturally and easily to you?

It might be gardening, cooking, writing, decluttering and organizing, styling bomb outfits, creating a custom face cream or confidently strutting across a stage and speaking in front of a crowd. You can take something that comes effortlessly to you, and this could be the seed of a million-dollar company.

What are the things you used to be really good at when you were a child?

Growing up changes us a lot, but our childhood can tell us a lot about ourselves. If there's something you used to be good at when you were younger, chances are you're still really good at it now. This childhood talent could be your Million Dollar Value, that "thing" that has the potential to make you millions of dollars.

What are the things you used to get in trouble for when you were growing up?

As a child, I always got in trouble for talking too much. Every report card would say, "Rachel is an excellent student, and she would have gotten even higher marks if she could learn to talk less." Well, guess who gets paid very well to talk and share all the ideas and thoughts in her head now? My natural ability to never shut up is making me millions. What about you?

What are the last three compliments you received?

Do you routinely get praised for how incredibly neat you are? Ding! Natural talent alert! You might be the future CEO of a million-dollar home-organizing empire, the next Marie Kondo. Do friends thank you for being so supportive and encouraging, their biggest cheerleader? Bang the money gong! You might have exactly what it takes to run a seven-figure fitness studio or life-coaching practice.

Make a list of valuable, helpful things you've done for your employer and/or clients in the past, including any freebie work you've done.

You saved your last employer tons of money? Write that down! You improved a janky system and vastly increased productivity in your department? Put that down, too. Lawsuits avoided. Sales achieved. Results your clients got, thanks to you. Put it all down on the list.

_____

_____

_____

_____

_____

_____

_____

If you had to take a guess, how would you fill in the following blank? "I have a hunch that I could make a million dollars doing _____."

_____

_____

_____

_____

_____

_____

_____

_____

MILLION DOLLAR ACTION

Find your Million Dollar Offer.

What could you offer to the world that is extremely valuable? What is something you could do that has the potential to make you millions of dollars?

I call this a Million Dollar Offer. It's a product, service, program, or experience that has the potential to make you a very rich woman.

A Million Dollar Offer is not just any old thing. It has to meet certain criteria.

1. It has to be something you are good at and love doing.

Otherwise you will get bored and give up. Making a million dollars from your offer will require commitment. It's easy to commit to something you love. You don't have to rely on discipline when you are doing work that you enjoy.

2. It has to be something that people actually want.

People want better sleep. People want more free time. People want a beautiful home. People want delicious beverages. And so on. Make sure your offer is something that people want very much.

3. It has to be scalable.

Your Million Dollar Offer needs to be something you can scale so that you can serve more people and make more money. This could mean: hiring a team to help you, training and certifying people to do your unique method, creating a program that hundreds of people can do online, franchising and having locations in multiple cities, and so on. Think: BIG.

4. It has to provide some kind of transformation for your client, customer, or employer.

It must take them from Point A to Point B.

For instance, Point A (your client is frustrated and confused about how to invest in commercial real estate) and then Point B (after working with you, your client is empowered and just made his or her first investment. Victory!)

Can you think of a Million Dollar Offer that matches all those criteria for you? Write down ideas.

If you are not sure, review everything you wrote previously—things that come naturally to you, things you were good at as a kid, things you get compliments for, valuable things you've done in the past for your employers and colleagues. This may give you some clues as to what your Million Dollar Offer could be.

EXTRA CREDIT

Discover more about your strengths by completing an assessment.

Maybe you feel like, "I am still not sure what I bring to the table, or what I could offer to the world that is extremely valuable."

If you still feel unsure, do an assessment like StrengthsFinder, DISC, or Kolbe to learn more about your natural strengths. You can take each of these assessments online for free or a small fee. The assessments take about 30 minutes or less, and you will receive an instant report on your personality and natural strengths once the assessment is complete.

You can do this on the phone, via email, or in person. Or talk to five people who know you well and ask them to share what they think about you. Talk to friends, colleagues, clients, mentors. Ask them to complete the following statements about you.

One of [your name]'s strongest skills is _____

_____

One thing that [your name] can do that is incredibly valuable is _____

_____

When I'm around [your name], I feel _____

_____

I feel that [your name] has a gift for _____

_____

When [your name] is thriving, excelling, and doing her absolute best work, this looks like _____

_____

I think [your name] could start a million-dollar company doing _____

_____

_____.

Notice what people say about you. Sometimes, other people can see your genius and your Million Dollar Value more clearly than you do.

GRADUATION CHECKLIST

To graduate from this section—"Million Dollar Value"—and move along to the next section of the workbook, complete the following items.

Be sure to check off every item before moving to the next section.

- ☐ Answer the Million Dollar Questions on page 106 of this workbook.

- ☐ Spend time thinking about this big, important question: "What could I offer to the world that is extremely valuable?"

- ☐ Find your Million Dollar Offer and make sure it matches the criteria laid out on page 109. If you're not sure about your Million Dollar Offer yet, that's okay. Brainstorm some possibilities and write them down.

- ☐ Extra credit: Do an assessment like StrengthsFinder or DISC, or ask five people to state what they appreciate and admire about you; what they think your Million Dollar Value might be.

- ☐ Highly recommended: Open the book *We Should All Be Millionaires*. Read the chapter "Million Dollar Value" to go even deeper into this topic.

- ☐ Fill in the blank: "I could see myself running a million-dollar company doing _____."

MILLION
DOLLAR PRICING

*Y*ou're probably undercharging severely for your labor. It's time to charge a lot more. In fact, you should double your rates.

KEY POINTS TO KNOW

Due to imposter syndrome, systemic racism, and misogyny, you are probably undercharging for your labor . . . severely.

You're offering bargain-basement pricing when you ought to be charging top dollar. In doing so, over the course of your career, you're literally leaving millions on the table.

You can (and should) raise your prices significantly, whether you are an entrepreneur or an employee.

Consider the tremendous value[4] you provide to your employer or clients.

Do you help your boss prepare for presentations so that he can shine, instead of looking foolish and unprepared? Do you help your clients recover from infidelity and save their marriages? Do you give your customers hair color that is so stunning, their confidence literally triples?

What you provide is extremely valuable. Your pricing needs to reflect this. Start charging based on the value you provide, rather than charging by-the-hour.

If you're an entrepreneur, double your prices. Update your website. Let clients know, "Here are my rates." You don't need to provide a big explanation about why you are doing it. Just do it.

The very next client or customer who inquires about working with you, tell them the new (higher) rate. "It's $3,000 per trademark." "Packages start

---

[4] Flip back to the previous section, Million Dollar Value, to refresh your memory on this.

at $5,000." "The deluxe skin care collection is $200." State the new number coolly and calmly, as if it has always been this way.

If you're an employee, put together a new-and-improved compensation package for yourself. Prepare a proposal with your new increased salary and benefits. Back up your request with evidence of how you have already helped the company increase revenue and hit other important company goals. Show your boss how saying yes to this new package will improve company performance.

When you're earning double, your life improves dramatically. Your friends and family reap the benefits, too. They get to enjoy a calmer, happier, and more prosperous version of you.

Earning double means you can do more for your community, too. You'll have a much larger impact on the world when you are earning more.

NOTES

_____

_____

_____

_____

_____

_____

_____

_____

_____

_____

_____

_____

_____

MILLION DOLLAR QUESTION

What would you do if you had a million dollars right now?

Would you buy a new home? Hire a full-time nanny? Take your entire family on a fabulous vacation? Something else?

Make a list of everything you would do and be if you had $1,000,000 in your bank account right now. Read your list out loud. Imagine just how much you could accomplish with that money. Let this list motivate you to double your prices today.

Double your prices.

If you're employed, it's time to ask your boss for a bigger salary. How much bigger? Double. Follow these guidelines to prepare for a successful conversation and inspire your boss to say, "Yes!"

If you're self-employed, take a look at the following guidelines, because many of them apply to you, too. Just change the word "boss" to "client" in your head as you go along. And then, self-employed folks, be sure to look at page 125 to see a special template just for you.

1. Make a list of recent accomplishments.

Over the last few months, how have you made your boss's life easier, or how have you made the company stronger?

Did you save the company a bunch of money? Did you fix a janky system? Did you keep the team strong and calm during an emotionally difficult time?

Or have you been going above and beyond the scope of whatever you were originally hired to do? For instance, maybe you were initially hired to manage a team of four, but now you're managing ten people?

Make a list of (at least) five valuable, helpful, or impressive things you've done recently.

_____

_____

_____

_____

_____

_____

_____

_____

_____

2. Decide exactly what you want.

Do you want to increase your salary? By how much? (I hope it's double.)

And/or is there something else you want, like a flexible schedule, more vacation time, a beautiful corner office, profit-share of the company, or something else?

If you don't ask, you don't get. You need to be willing to ask for exactly what you want. Write it down to make sure you have your requests crystal clear.

_____

_____

_____

_____

_____

_____

_____

_____

_____

_____

3. If you want to ask for a bigger salary, brainstorm and figure out two or three paths to make this happen.

For instance, if you are currently paid $50,000 per year and you want $100,000, there are a couple possible paths to reach that $100,000 mark.

One option is your employer doubles your salary. Simple as that.

Another option is your employer increases your salary from $50,000 to $70,000, and then you work out an agreement where you can earn the remaining $30,000 through a combination of monthly bonuses and/or profit-sharing in the company when you hit certain performance targets.

Another option might be that you get paid $80,000 per year, plus you can use the business location any weekends you want (free of charge) as an event space to teach seminars that will bring at least $20,000 in the door, if not more.

Decide what number you want—whether it's $100,000 or $200,000 or $500,000 or more—and then figure out a couple possibilities that you could propose to your employer.

That way, you can work together to find a path that works on both sides. Get creative. Write down two or three paths to your ideal salary.

4. Schedule a time to meet with your employer.

Asking for a bigger salary might require more than just a quick email.

A phone, video, or face-to-face meeting is probably the best route for this one. And it might take more than one meeting.

First, write down what times would work best for your schedule. Then, send those options to your employer so you can set it up.

_____

_____

_____

_____

_____

_____

_____

_____

_____

_____

_____

_____

_____

_____

_____

_____

_____

_____

5. Create a conversation plan for the first meeting.

If you're not sure where to start, use the conversation template that follows to give you some structure.

CONVERSATION TEMPLATE: EMPLOYEE ASKING FOR DOUBLE

Here's an example of how your conversation with your employer could go.

Hey, thanks so much for meeting with me today. I appreciate your time.

First off, I really enjoy working here. The company's mission is very meaningful to me, and I feel emotionally connected to the work we do every day.

Over the last few months, the scope of my work has expanded quite a bit. While I was initially hired to be the assistant to the director of communications, I'm now doing quite a bit more—including writing and developing content for online educational programs, managing launches and other projects, supervising three interns, and training junior writers who join the communications department team.

A few recent accomplishments, just from the last month:

- Wrote new website language and supervised the company's website relaunch, which led to a huge spike in new email list subscribers—more than five thousand newsletter subscribers in one week.

- Wrote sales emails and managed our most recent product launch, which generated 300 percent more than last year's launch.

- Wrote nearly all the content for our newest e-course, which won a prestigious Webby Award in the education category. This award led to media buzz in *Forbes* and *Time*.

My role has expanded. My contributions have increased. I'd like to find a way for my compensation to increase as well.

Here's my current compensation package, workplace environment, and schedule:

- $50,000 per year

- two weeks paid vacation

- cubicle workspace

- working from the office headquarters five days per week

- intern supporting me five hours per week

Here's the new package I propose, starting July 1:

- $100,000 per year

- three weeks paid vacation

- office with a door: more privacy and fewer interruptions so I can do even higher-quality work more efficiently

- option to work from home one day per week

- intern supporting me fifteen hours per week

- one professional training program each year, all training fees/airfare/hotel/expenses included, to continue developing my leadership skills

- opportunity to speak onstage at this year's conference. (I have a presentation in mind that I'd like to share with you.)

Let me know if that works for you.
And if you want to think this over, and then have a follow-up meeting to discuss things further, that's great. Let me know.

Thank you!

6. Prior to the meeting, do something that makes you feel like a million bucks.

This is the moment to get your hair done, put on your power suit, wear grandma's heirloom jewelry to feel connected to your ancestors (make Gram Gram proud!) so you can go into the room (or Zoom) feeling your best.

Write down what you'll do to get ready and feel powerful before asking for your raise.

CONVERSATION TEMPLATE: IF YOU'RE SELF-EMPLOYED, ANNOUNCE YOUR NEW, HIGHER PRICES

Use this template to notify a client that your prices are increasing. You can use this language in an email, a phone conversation, a Zoom meeting, or whatever makes the most sense to you.

(You can also raise your prices without announcing it. Just do it. Sometimes, it is more powerful to simply update your website and put the new rates without any fuss or fanfare, rather than make a big deal about it. Trust your gut to determine whether to announce it or not.)

Hi, Tonia,

I wanted to say thank you again for hiring me earlier this year. It was such a joy to work with you.

Exciting news: I've made a few upgrades to serve my clients at an even higher level. Here are three upgrades I wanted you to know about:

1. Online booking

   From now on, you can choose an appointment and pay online. No more emailing back and forth to figure out a good time. Here's where to book online: *[provide link].*

2. New pricing

   I'm rolling out new pricing that goes into effect on January 1.
   Photo package (twenty photos): $2,000
   Photo and video package (twenty photos plus one-minute promo video): $3,500

3. New perks

   I love pampering my clients with the best things in life.
   When you purchase a package, you get a bonus gift—a snail-mail box

full of nourishing goodies shipped to your home. Take a sneak peek here: *[provide link]*. It's so good.

Thank you! I appreciate having you as a client. If you have any questions, email anytime.

Wishing you a beautiful month. Let's talk soon!

NOTES

_____

_____

_____

_____

_____

_____

_____

_____

_____

_____

_____

_____

_____

_____

_____

EXTRA CREDIT

Stop saying Broke Ass Affirmations to yourself. Start speaking to yourself like a millionaire.

Choose a Million Dollar Affirmation from the following list. Repeat it to yourself daily for one week or until it feels true and real.

Broke Ass Affirmation

My clients are broke and don't have enough money to pay my current fee, let alone a higher fee.

Million Dollar Affirmation

There are plenty of wonderful clients who are willing and able to pay me what I deserve. I just need to get out there and find them. I can and I will.

Broke Ass Affirmation

If I raise my prices, my clients will complain.

Million Dollar Affirmation

If I raise my prices, my ideal clients (the ones who truly respect me and value my skills) will support me. They will pay the higher fee without batting an eye. Plus, I will attract more ideal clients who are delightful to serve.

Broke Ass Affirmation

I will raise my prices . . . eventually. Maybe in a year or two. Not now.

Million Dollar Affirmation

I will raise my prices . . . today. I have been undercharging for years, and the time is now for that pattern to end.

Broke Ass Affirmation

It would be greedy to double my prices.

Million Dollar Affirmation

It would be smart to double my prices. Once I'm earning more, I can deliver an even better experience to my clients. Everyone wins.

Broke Ass Affirmation

My clients don't understand why it's valuable to hire me or pay me. People just don't "get" what I do.

Million Dollar Affirmation

It's my job to educate potential clients about why it's a great move to hire me and the results they can expect. I can do this!

Broke Ass Affirmation

I don't want to be too expensive.

Million Dollar Affirmation

I can't wait to be expensive! My skills are valuable. My time is a luxury commodity. I want to be the crème de la crème of my industry, not a discount-bargain-bin option.

Broke Ass Affirmation

It's really complicated to raise my prices.

Million Dollar Affirmation

It's really *not* complicated to raise my prices. I can go to my website or payment app, type in a new higher number, and click "update." Done. I don't need to overcomplicate this. It can be simple.

Broke Ass Affirmation

I just don't know how much to charge. I can't figure it out.

Million Dollar Affirmation

I know exactly how much to charge. I will take my previous rate and double it. Boom. Done.

Broke Ass Affirmation

I have a nine-to-five job working for somebody else. Unless my boss decides to give me a raise, there's no realistic way for me to earn more.

Million Dollar Affirmation

I have a nine-to-five job working for somebody else . . . and there are lots of ways I can earn more. I can ask for a raise. I can ask for a bonus. I can ask for profit-sharing in the company. I can start a side hustle. I have skills, and I have plenty of options.

Broke Ass Affirmation

I might turn into a completely different person once I have more money.

Million Dollar Affirmation

My wealthiest self is my most authentic self—the highest expression of all I can be.

GRADUATION CHECKLIST

To graduate from this section—"Million Dollar Pricing"—and move along to the next section of the workbook, complete the following items.
   Be sure to check off every item before moving to the next section.

   ☐ Answer the Million Dollar Questions on page 117 of this workbook.

   ☐ Double. Your. Prices. Whether you are self-employed or an employee, double your fee or salary and do it now. We provide guidelines starting on page 118 to help you do this successfully.

☐ If you are terrified to double your price, find a money-buddy who pledges to do it with you. Pick a date and time. Pledge to "do the scary thing" (update the website, email the boss, and so on) at the exact same moment together. Give each other emotional support and do not let each other chicken out! 3 . . . 2 . . . 1 . . . *double that price*!

☐ Extra credit: Read the Million Dollar Affirmations to strengthen your mindset and keep your attitude on the right track. You'll find several starting on page 127.

☐ Highly recommended: Open the book *We Should All Be Millionaires*. Read the chapter "Million Dollar Pricing" to go even deeper into this topic.

☐ Fill in the blank, "Once I am earning double, I can _____

_____

_____

_____

_____

_____

_____

_____

_____

_____

_____

_____

_____

_____."

MILLION
DOLLAR TEAM

*T*o climb Mount Millionaire, you need a team. Start by hiring a personal assistant five hours per week. This alone will change your life. Mastering delegation is the key to financial and time freedom.

KEY POINTS TO KNOW

Show me a room of a hundred millionaires. I can guarantee, none of those people attained a seven-figure net worth all by themselves with no help. Millionaires understand the importance of building a team and learning how to delegate.

You think Oprah, Beyoncé, or Michelle Obama do every single task all by themselves? You think they're staying up until 11:00 p.m. to proofread emails, send invoices, or do a late-night run to FedEx in their jammies to scan something real quick? No, they are not. And neither should you.

Now is the time to begin assembling your Million Dollar Team—and yes, you need to start doing this before you're a millionaire, not after.

Even if your annual income is peanuts compared to what you'd like to be earning, you need to build a team. Hiring help will help you earn more. The sooner you make your first hire, the better.

For most people, this looks like hiring a personal assistant or virtual assistant (part-time) to clear time-clogging tasks off your plate.

This person can start handling personal and business tasks (laundry, errands, scheduling appointments, answering emails, research, fact-checking, proofreading, and so much more) to free up twenty to thirty hours of your time every week.

This will change your life in profound ways.

With all that extra time, you can focus on money-generating activities like raising your prices, finding more clients, increasing your visibility through media appearances, writing a book, or zeroing in on a genius idea that's going to make you millions and bringing that idea to the marketplace.

You can also use your newfound free time to rest, take care of your body, spend time with people you love, and savor the beautiful life that you're working so hard to create.

After hiring a personal assistant, you may decide to expand your team by hiring a marketing assistant, salesperson, or perhaps "duplicating yourself" and hiring another attorney, another designer, another stylist, and so on, so that your company can serve more clients with excellence and you can scale your revenue.

Who you decide to hire will depend on your profession and goals. But one thing is certain: No matter what you do for a living, and whether you are self-employed or not, you must learn how to hire and delegate.

Learning to delegate is an essential step toward becoming a millionaire.

NOTES

MILLION DOLLAR QUESTIONS

Imagine you have a fantastic personal assistant who is ecstatic for the opportunity to work with/for you.

Perhaps this person is a recent high school or college graduate, new in the workforce, and absolutely stoked to have a cool boss like you.

What are the first ten things you want to delegate to this person? Make a list.

This list could include: chores you loathe doing, time-consuming errands, tedious administrative tasks, double-checking and proofreading, researching to find opportunities for you. Really, anything you want.

1. _____

2. _____

3. _____

4. _____

5. _____

6. _____

7. _____

8. _____

9. _____

10. _____

Once you've delegated those ten things to your new assistant, how much time will this free up in your life every week? Take a guesstimate. Ten hours per week, fifteen, twenty, more?

_____

_____

_____

_____

_____

_____

_____

_____

_____

What could you do with all that newfound time? What are some important money-generating priorities that you'd be free to focus on?

_____

_____

_____

_____

_____

_____

_____

_____

_____

_____

_____

_____

MILLION DOLLAR ACTION

Start your Million Dollar Team. Make your first hire.

Here's how to hire a personal assistant or PA. (You can use these same guidelines to hire other roles, too.)

Step 1. Write down the personality traits, skills, and talents of your dream personal assistant.

This list will serve you well when you are deciding between your top candidates.

Step 2. Write a job description for the role.

We've included a sample job description for you on page 141, if you need some inspiration.

_____

_____

_____

_____

_____

_____

_____

_____

_____

_____

Step 3. Get the description out into the world.

Post the job description on Craigslist, community forums, and job boards. Or maybe you already know someone who might be perfect for the job—like your friend's niece, a college student you know, or someone else. Reach out and ask if they'd be interested.

Write down where you will post the description and/or who you will reach out to below.

_____

_____

_____

_____

_____

_____

Step 4. Review résumés and choose the top three or four candidates to interview.

When you're ready, list your top candidates here.

_____

_____

_____

_____

_____

_____

_____

_____

_____

Step 5. Have your top two candidates do a "test day."

During the test day, you can pay them to handle a few tasks for you before you commit to hiring one. This allows you to determine who is a good fit.

When you're ready, write down which tasks you'll be assigning them for the "test day."

_____

_____

_____

_____

_____

_____

_____

_____

Step 6. Make the offer to your top candidate and provide an official offer letter.

When you're ready, write up the offer letter below.

_____

_____

_____

_____

_____

_____

_____

_____

_____

_____

_____

_____

_____

_____

_____

_____

_____

_____

_____

_____

_____

_____

Step 7. Celebrate! You got yourself a personal assistant!

SAMPLE JOB DESCRIPTION

PERSONAL ASSISTANT NEEDED [THREE DAYS PER WEEK]

Busy business owner and mom of four looking for a great, local, personal assistant. I would love to find a detail-oriented and experienced personal assistant who loves organization, enjoys hanging out with kids as well as generally helping out with whatever is needed.

Duties include:

- Scheduling personal appointments for myself and the children (doctor appts, lawyer appts, school volunteering, playdates, and so on)

- Booking travel arrangements (flights, hotel, car service, and so on)

- Managing my inbox including drafting and sending emails

- Keep my spaces organized, including office, closet, files, and so on

- Managing returns and other errands such as shopping, picking up dry-cleaning, post office, and so on

- Sort mail, deliveries, and so on

- Order, wrap, and ship gifts

- Coordinate scheduling, travel, events, and so on with my nanny as well as my business team

- Packing and unpacking before or after travel

- Light cleaning when needed

- Occasional help with the kids when needed—driving them to appointments, picking them up from school, helping out with birthday parties, holding the baby while I do my makeup (LOL, but not kidding), and so on

- Occasionally travel with me on business trips

An ideal schedule would be 2:00–6:00 p.m., Monday, Wednesday, and Friday.

If you're punctual, reliable, a nonsmoker, and a self-starter (plus can craft a great email), I'd love to talk to you.

Please reply to this ad (either in writing or with a quick video on your phone) with:

- Your name

- What city you live in

- Your phone number

- What days and times during the week you are available

- Why you'd be great for this position

- What you do on the other days of the week (other jobs? parenting? school?)

Please use the word "AVOCADO" in the subject line of your email (to ensure you've read this entire post). Thank you!

How Much to Pay Your PA

For a part-time personal assistant, $20 to $30 per hour would be a good place to start. Start with five hours per week and go from there.

You can also work with your PA to develop a payment system that's based on results or value provided rather than hours on the clock.

For instance, if your PA can accomplish the list of weekly tasks in ten hours rather than twenty hours, amazing, and you can still pay them the same amount regardless of how long it took.

That way, you're encouraging your PA to get things done efficiently (and get that coin!) rather than just "filling hours." Pay your PA the same way you'd like to get paid—based on value, not necessarily time.

If you make financial decisions along with a partner or spouse, schedule a time to sit down and talk.

When I tell people to build out their team and hire household support, one objection I often get is: "I'm totally down with the idea of hiring help, but my partner/spouse/roomie won't get it."

If that's you, then sit down with your cohabitant and have an exciting conversation about why you want to hire help, exactly how much it will cost, the benefits of doing this, and why this is a win-win situation for the entire household.

If you don't know how to have this type of conversation, follow the script that follows, and adjust it based on your situation.

This would probably be best as a face-to-face conversation (assuming you live together and share household expenses) rather than an email or a video meeting.

NOTES

SUGGESTED SCRIPT

To discuss division of household labor with your partner, spouse, roommates, or whoever you live with.

Hey! I was hoping we could sit down and have a conversation. I have some exciting ideas I wanted to share with you.

Let's talk tomorrow morning, after we've slept and we've got fresh brains. Cool?

[The next morning, after you've both enjoyed a good night's sleep, had your coffee, and feel revived and ready for the day . . .]

Okay, so I did a really interesting time tracking exercise this last week. I was curious to find out how much time I typically spend every week doing household chores—laundry, vacuuming, mopping, making the beds, grocery shopping, cooking, cleaning up the kitchen, putting away dishes, and other tasks like that.

I downloaded an app called Toggl and tracked my time for one week. Wanna guess the number?

[Partner guesses]

It was fifteen hours in one week, which adds up to 780 hours per year. *[Obviously change "fifteen" to whatever it actually was for you.]*

[Partner gasps in shock, and says, "Nooo! That's awful! You are my queen, and this is outrageous!")

I know, right? 780 hours is so much time! This got me thinking, if I had an extra 780 hours of free time every year, what could I do with that time? I mean, for starters, I would love to . . .

- Work on my career [start my side hustle / grow my business / earn more money]

- Invest way more time into my health [yoga / meditation / gym time / daily walks]

- Spend quality time with you [and the kids!]

- And so many other things.

An extra 780 hours per year would significantly change my energy levels, my health, my ability to work and earn more money—it would change my life. Really, both our lives.

[Partner agrees—"Yes, it definitely would."]

So, here's what I'm thinking: I would like to hire someone to help around the house. I propose that we start small—for instance, get a personal assistant who can help with laundry, meal preparation, and running errands. We could start by hiring someone five hours a week at $20 an hour. So, that's $100 per week, $400 per month.

[Partner might say, "Great, when do we start?" or "But how can we pay for that?"]

I have a plan to pay for this!

[Explain your plan—you'll sell a consulting package, you'll find two more clients, you'll negotiate for a raise at work, you'll sell some furniture, whatever you intend to do.]

Hiring someone costs money, that's true. But I feel confident that this investment will pay for itself many times over. This will free up so much time and energy and enable me to [strengthen my business / hugely increase my income]. Plus, more quality time for us to [snuggle together / have amazing sex / go on hikes / do anything besides fold laundry, hooray!]

Are you cool with this plan?

[Let your partner express any hesitations they might have, and address each one. At this point, you can agree to a plan and wrap up the conversation. Done. Hooray! Or if you feel like you need to keep discussing things a bit more, here are some great questions to discuss with your partner.]

- Around the house, what are some things you really enjoy doing? (Cool, keep doing that stuff.)

- Around the house, what are some things you don't enjoy doing? (Okay, let's delegate these tasks to someone else.)

- What kind(s) of helper(s) do we want? (House cleaner, nanny, personal assistant, virtual assistant, gardener/lawn care, pet care, what else?)

- How many hours per week?

- How much will that cost? (Look at websites like TaskRabbit.com and upwork.com to find pricing.)

- How are we gonna get those funds? What's the plan?

- When can we start?

EXTRA CREDIT

In addition to hiring an assistant, what are some other roles you want to hire soon? Write down the next three roles you will hire.

For instance: "In the near future I want to hire a personal chef, a nanny, and a customer service specialist for my business."

1. _____

2. _____

3. _____

GRADUATION CHECKLIST

To graduate from this section—"Million Dollar Team"—and move along to the next section of the workbook, complete the following items.

Be sure to check off every item before moving to the next section.

☐ Answer the Million Dollar Questions on page 135 of this workbook.

- ☐ Make your first hire. Most likely, this will be a part-time personal assistant who can clear myriad tasks off your plate and free up tons of time. Use the steps and sample job description that we provide starting on page 137 to do this successfully.

- ☐ If applicable to your situation, have a conversation with your spouse, significant other, or other person about who you want to hire, how much it will cost, and when you'd like to start. Use the conversation script on page 144.

- ☐ Extra credit: Start dreaming bigger. Make a list of the next three people you want to hire once you've got a PA. Write down these roles on page 146.

- ☐ Highly recommended: Open the book *We Should All Be Millionaires*. Read the chapter "Million Dollar Team" to go even deeper into this topic.

- ☐ Fill in the blank, "I am so excited to start building my Million Dollar Team because _____

_____

_____

_____

_____

_____

_____

_____

_____

_____

_____

_____."

MILLION DOLLAR SYSTEMS

*S*et up Million Dollar Systems to track your money, manage your money, and bring attention to your money. Your money is not going to grow if you refuse to look at it.

KEY POINTS TO KNOW

Even if you feel ashamed, disorganized, and sloppy when it comes to your money, here's the good news: It is never too late to create systems and get things on track.

Yes, even if you have massive debt, a negative net worth, a painfully low credit score, shoeboxes full of disorganized receipts, and filing your tax paperwork feels a little bit like throwing spaghetti against the wall and praying that it's gonna stick—even if that's your situation, things are not hopeless. You can get your financial house in order. And you can start now.

Now is the time to set up Million Dollar Systems for managing your money. It's time to grow up and glow up!

At a minimum, you need to track your net worth, credit score, and daily spending, and go to Money Church[5] every week. If you're self-employed, you need to go legit, form a business entity (such as LLC, S-Corp, and so on), and open a business checking account.

By getting your systems in place, you will be proud of yourself, organized, capable, like a real boss instead of a hot mess. This boosts your confidence and changes the way you carry yourself in the world. You'll attract more clients, more opportunities, and more money once you've got systems in place.

---

[5] More on this in a moment.

Commit to paying attention to your money, even if there's not much of it yet. Create systems to track your money and treat it with the respect it deserves.

Last: Shift the way you think about debt. While some personal finance gurus insist that debt is the devil and should be avoided at all costs, I disagree. Debt can be a tool that you can use strategically to increase your earning potential. Debt is not something to be ashamed of. It often represents an investment you've made in yourself.

NOTES

MILLION DOLLAR QUESTIONS

What are some financial systems that you currently have in place? For instance, do you check your credit score regularly? Do you automatically contribute to a retirement fund monthly? What are some things you do consistently?

What's an area of your financial world that feels messy, neglected, and you're not proud of it? This could be tax paperwork, avoiding looking at your bank account balances because it feels uncomfortable, or perhaps philanthropy/giving back (you keep meaning to do it, but don't really have a system in place yet).

Imagine that you have clear, excellent financial systems in place. Systems to track what's coming in and going out. Systems to pay bills on time. Systems to invest and make your money grow. Systems to organize receipts and other paperwork. Everything is legit, orderly, pristine, correct. If the IRS decided to audit you, they would gasp and say: "We have never seen such beautiful organization and systems! This is wonderful! Well done!"

If this was your situation, how would you feel? How would your life change if you had these kinds of systems in place?

MILLION DOLLAR ACTION

Create systems for the financial life you want, not the one you have.

You've heard the expression, "Dress for the job you want, not the job you have." Same thing applies to your money.

Plan ahead and create systems for the financial life you want, not the one you've currently got. This means to start behaving as if you have a million dollars net worth. Behave with the assumption that, one day, you will.

At a bare minimum, these are the financial systems you need to have in place. You don't have to do all of these things today. But, commit to doing at least one of these things in the next seven days. And commit to setting up everything on this list in the next hundred days.

Yes, you can.

- Hire a professional tax preparer and meet with them regularly. Once or twice a year, minimum.

- Hire a professional bookkeeper and/or get bookkeeping software (like YNAB or Empower for your personal finances and Xero or QuickBooks for your small business finances).

- Hire a professional financial planner who can help you prepare for retirement, make investments, and set big-picture money goals. Meet with this person regularly, once or twice a year, minimum.

- Hire a money coach who can help you clear emotional blocks, set specific goals, and check in with you regularly to make sure you are doing the things you promised to do. Meet with your money coach weekly (ideally) for ten to twelve weeks and you will make massive progress. (At Hello Seven, we have a team of Certified Hello Seven Coaches that can help you with this. Go to helloseven.co/coach to learn more.)

- Check your credit score. Do this monthly. (Your credit card company or bank will probably give you an updated score every thirty days for free.)

- Create a spreadsheet with a list of every debt you currently have including the total amount, interest rate, and monthly payment. Update this spreadsheet each month as you make payments. Look at this debt tracker each week, even if it's uncomfortable. Doing so will help you take action and make progress.

- Look at your bank account(s) to see what's coming in, and what's going out. Do this daily.

- Track your net worth. This is all the assets you've got, minus whatever debt you owe. Do this weekly.

- Brainstorm ideas for generating extra income. I call these Million Dollar Ideas. Every week write down twenty-five ideas to create extra income that can pay off one of your debts, allow you to purchase something you want, or allow you to invest the extra money. Creating a habit of brainstorming Million Dollar Ideas will train your brain to see moneymaking opportunities everywhere you look.

- If you are self-employed, find out what you need to do to go legit and run your business like a pro. This may include getting a particular license for your region or state, getting insurance, filing to form an LLC or S-Corp or another business structure, opening a business checking account, and more.

- If you are self-employed and based in the United States, find out when your quarterly estimated tax payments are due. Put the due dates into your calendar. Remember to send payments on time. You can usually do this online.

- Automate as many payments as you can to simplify your life. Phone bill, health insurance, any regular payments that happen weekly or monthly. Set those up on auto-pay so you don't have to worry about it. Less clutter in your brain.

- If you share household finances with your spouse/partner, schedule a recurring appointment when you sit down together to set money goals and discuss: "What's something that would upgrade our life? What do we want to buy? Who are some people we want to hire? What's the plan to pay for it? When can we start?" Do this monthly.

- Do an annual money review. Once a year, obviously. See page 204 of this workbook for tips on how to do this.

You may be wondering, *"But when am I going to do all those things?"*

My advice: Schedule a weekly appointment on your calendar and call it Money Church.

Or call it Hot Money Date or Me 'n My Benjamins or whatever name you want.

At least sixty to ninety minutes. Every week. This is your time to light a candle, play your favorite music, and do all the weekly steps we just discussed (check your credit score, look at your accounts, look at your debt, and so on). Like a weekly money review.

Money Church is also a great opportunity to take stock of what's been happening in your life lately. Reflect on the last week. What are some Million Dollar Decisions you made that you want to celebrate? What are some Broke Ass Decisions you (accidentally) made? What are some money-generating ideas that you could implement soon?

See page 201 of this workbook for more information on Money Church and how to do it successfully. Money Church needs to be a nonnegotiable part of your financial routine.

EXTRA CREDIT

Write a thank-you letter to your debt.

So many people feel intense shame about debt. This shame can build and build, eventually becoming so massive and cumbersome that it's like a solid brick wall blocking you from achieving your financial goals.

It's difficult to get dressed to impress, pitch yourself to a new client, increase your prices with confidence, or stride into a meeting with a financial planner when you are burdened with ten thousand pounds of shame.

You need to shatter the shame-wall and let it go, so that it doesn't block you from doing the things you need to do.

Reframe your debt. Instead of hating your debt or feeling ashamed for your debt, flip your attitude completely around. Say "thank you" to your debt. Express gratitude for everything that debt has brought into your life, whether it's an experience, a possession, an education, or an expensive-but-valuable lesson.

Write a letter and say "thank you" to your debt—for the college degree, the career possibilities, the beautiful coat, the fantastic birthday dinner with friends, the trip to Paris, the wedding gift for your sister, or whatever else this debt allowed you to have.

Dear Debt,

Thank you for . . .

_____

_____

_____

_____

_____

_____

_____

_____

_____

_____

_____

_____

_____

_____

_____

_____

_____

_____

_____

_____

Sincerely,

Me

The more you can view your debt with gratitude, the lighter it feels, and the less it clutters up your brain. Instead of obsessing about your debt, get obsessed with earning more money. Focus on generating more, and soon, the debt will be paid off.

GRADUATION CHECKLIST

To graduate from this section—"Million Dollar Systems"—and move along to the next section of the workbook, complete the following items.
Be sure to check off every item before moving to the next section.

- ☐ Answer the Million Dollar Questions on page 153 of this workbook.

- ☐ Review the list of financial systems that you need to have, at bare minimum, found on page 155. Circle the ones that you haven't set up yet. Get those systems in place.

- [ ] Schedule your first Money Church appointment. You can call it Money Temple, Money Date, Money Time, whatever you want. Make this a weekly appointment. Look at page 157 to see what to do during Money Church.

- [ ] Extra credit: Write a thank-you letter to your debt, expressing gratitude for the positive things it has brought into your life. Shift your perspective. Release the shame.

- [ ] Highly recommended: Open the book *We Should All Be Millionaires*. Read the chapter "Million Dollar Systems" to go even deeper into this topic.

- [ ] Fill in the blanks, "One system I already have is _____

_____

_____

_____

_____

_____

_____.

One system I need to establish is _____

_____

_____

_____

_____

_____

_____

_____."

A MILLION DOLLARS NOW

mpossible is only impossible until you do it. Then, pretty soon, "impossible" becomes your new normal. Pledge to do the $10k in 10 Days Challenge and prepare to astonish yourself. You are capable of earning more money whenever you want or need. You don't need to wait until later when conditions are "perfect." You have this ability right now.

KEY POINTS TO KNOW

A Black family in the White House. Walking on the moon. Earning $1 million in a single year. Or in a single month.

Everything feels impossible until, one day, somebody goes out and does it. Then it's no longer impossible, it's inspiring and attainable. Eventually, it becomes normal.

The best way to prove to yourself that you can do something is simply to do it.

You can read all the books in the world, but nothing increases your confidence like rolling up your sleeves and doing the dang thing.

I could preach to you: "You can do this! You are perfectly capable of making more money! A lot more!" for the next hundred hours, but you probably won't believe me until you see the evidence for yourself.

It's time to go create the proof that you need.

Do the $10k in 10 Days Challenge so you can prove to yourself that you are capable of making large sums of money in short periods of time, whenever you want.

The premise is very simple. Choose a start date. Then, get moving and go generate an extra $10,000 in just ten days.

You can sell services to clients, negotiate a raise at work, sell furniture you don't need, rent out your spare car—there are tons of options, and I'll give you a big list of ideas in just a moment. One way or another, your challenge is to rake those coins in the door.

You may already be thinking, "This sounds absolutely preposterous, and it will never work! There's no way I can earn that much money in just ten days!"

To that, I say—before you automatically decide that you can't do this—how about you just try? You may surprise yourself. Most of my clients do.

Completing the $10k in 10 Days Challenge will open the floodgates and unleash your inner millionaire.

You will complete this challenge and feel like, "Wow! Okay, I did that. What else can I do—$10,000 is just the beginning!"

The key is, you must push yourself to do a $10k in 10 Days Challenge *now*. Today, this week, within the next month at the very latest.

Do not delay. Do not convince yourself "I am not ready" or "I need a website first" or "I need to finish my PhD."

You do not need any of those things. You are ready. You have the intelligence, the creativity, everything you need to generate more money right now. You simply have to stop stalling and go do it.

NOTES

MILLION DOLLAR QUESTION

Imagine an extra $10,000 sitting in your bank account ten days from now. What would you do with that money? How would it feel? How would this change your life?

MILLION DOLLAR ACTION

Do the $10k in 10 Days Challenge.

You can do this challenge any time of year, starting on whatever day you choose.

The goal is to get an extra $10,000 into your bank account in ten days, in whatever way (or ways) you want. Rake in those coins! Read on for ideas and instructions.

How are you going to earn an extra $10,000? There are so many possibilities. You could:

- Finally launch that product, service, or program—you know, the one you've been tinkering with for months now.

- Forgive yourself for not using the treadmill/fancy stand mixer/ bicycle/inherited antique armoire/designer handbag, and sell it.

- Sell a mini challenge to your clients (like a seven-day fitness challenge, for example) with an upgrade offer at the end.

- Raise your prices immediately. This could mean notifying your current clients that the price is going up or asking your employer for a raise.

- Or raise your prices effective in thirty days—and offer current clients a way to purchase ahead at the current price. (For instance, tell your clients that they can prebook a package of six sessions right now at the "old" price.)

- Create an incentivized offer for your clients to pay the remainder of their contract now. (For instance, if you have a client who has committed to paying you $2,000 per month for the next six months, you could offer that client a special bonus if they pay the remaining balance—$12,000—right now. This bonus could be a free session, a special gift, or anything else you'd like to do.)

- Ask people to reimburse you. Maybe you paid for accommodations, a flight, gas, or training/education out-of-pocket, and your employer (or a client) was going to reimburse you later. Get reimbursed now.

- Follow up on those unpaid invoices. That one client who's thirty days late paying his invoice? Nudge him and make sure it gets paid.

- Circle back to a previous client or customer and see if it's time for a "refill." Perhaps that client would like to hire you again for another project or place another order. Get that repeat business.

- Create a short-term group offer that brings all your favorite clients together so you can try working with them in a group setting.

- You sold one of your offers to an awesome client? Circle back with an upsell. Maybe she wants to upgrade to a VIP package and work with you in a more elevated, luxurious way.

- Dust off an old product, freshen it with an update, and put it on sale for a limited time only.

- Rent out a spare room. Or that cabin your family has that no one uses. Or rent out your spare car on a website like Turo.com.

- Buy old furniture. Sand it down, paint it, and sell it on Craigslist for a profit.

- Negotiate bonus pay for that extra project you've been managing at work.

- Dog sit, babysit, or house-sit for your neighbors.

- Sell a workshop/training/seminar to a group you know would benefit from your expertise.

- Host a yard sale.

- Go on a cancellation spree, and free yourself from all the little monthly charges for services you don't use much (but definitely keep what sparks joy).

- Go to airbnb.com and create an Airbnb experience that tourists and staycationers can purchase online. You could offer guided nature hikes in your area, a cooking class, poetry workshop, a walking tour of your town's haunted historic buildings, or whatever you have the passion or expertise to do.

- Hunt for money that's rightfully yours. You might have unclaimed money owed to you due to a class action legal settlement, insurance refunds, an inheritance you didn't know about, tax refund, economic stimulus and emergency relief payments, or some other source of funds. Visit unclaimed.org. It can't hurt to check.

- Those are just a few money-generating options. See if you can brainstorm even more.

- When is your $10k in 10 Days Challenge going to happen? Pick specific dates. Make it real.

Are you aiming for $10,000? Less? More? Choose a number that feels exciting and doable, but also a stretch. For you, this might be $5,000 or $50,000 or $200,000. It depends. Remember: This is supposed to feel challenging. What number are you aiming for?

Brainstorm moneymaking ideas. Come up with at least ten ways that you could bring cash in the door quickly. (You've already written down dozens of moneymaking ideas previously in this workbook, so you've got a head start! Remember to peek at the list we provided on page 166 for some good ideas to get your wheels turning.)

1.

2.

3.

4.

5.

6.

7.

8.

9.

10.

Narrow your choices down to one to three ideas that feel exciting, fun, and that won't lock you into a long-term commitment.

Choose options that feel sexy, fun, exciting, speedy, and short term. The purpose of the $10k in 10 Days Challenge is to generate extra cash quickly, not lock yourself into a new full-time job or a twelve-month client commitment that you'll detest a few weeks later. On the previous list, circle up to three options you are going to take action on. Add additional notes here:

Who's on your cheerleading squad?

Pick three friends (or more!) to whom you'll announce your goal. You can tell them: "I'm doing something really exciting, and I want you to know!" They can do the $10k in 10 Days Challenge along with you, or they can provide support and pep talks from the sidelines. Write down who's in your squad.

Is there anything holding you back from earning more money right now?

For instance, maybe you feel like "I don't have time to do this" or "It would be better to wait until next summer" or "I need to finish my master's degree first." Write down the thing that is holding you back.

Whatever seems to be holding you back, choose a new attitude.

What is a Million Dollar Story you will say to yourself throughout this challenge? Write it down.

For instance: "I can create the time to do this." "It would be best to go for it now, not later." "I am already skilled enough, qualified enough, and prepared enough. I don't need to keep delaying. I am ready."

_____

_____

_____

_____

_____

_____

_____

Go forth and get that coin!

First, $10k in 10 Days. Then, $100,000. Then, $1 million. And beyond.

Celebrate your wins! Do a happy shmoney dance to celebrate every chunk of cash that you bring in the door. Treat yourself right—fun music, a celebratory beverage, a movie night, give yourself all the good vibes.

Whether you end up earning less than $10,000 or more than $10,000, either way, you've got additional money that you didn't have before! This is a win, no matter what.

Review and do it again

After completing your first $10k in 10 Days Challenge, review what happened. What worked great? What didn't go so well? What would you do differently next time? In the space below, write down what you learned while doing the $10k in 10 Days Challenge.

_____

_____

_____

_____

_____

_____

_____

_____

_____

_____

_____

Then, do it again.

Plan another $10k in 10 Days Challenge in the near future—and next time, dream even bigger. Could you shoot for $15,000? Or $20,000? More? The floodgates are open. There's no stopping you now!

Convince someone else to do the challenge with you. Help someone else rise while you're rising, too.

Don't want to do the challenge on your own? You're in luck. At my company, Hello Seven, we host a guided $10k in 10 Days Challenge several times a year. You'll be led through the challenge by Hello Seven Coaches and along with many other folks just like you. Instant Million Dollar Squad. Sign up to join our next guided $10k in 10 Days Challenge here: helloseven.co/10k.

GRADUATION CHECKLIST

To graduate from this section—"A Million Dollars Now"—complete the following items.

Be sure to check off every item before moving to the next section.

☐ Answer the Million Dollar Question on page 165 of this workbook.

☐ Plan your $10k in 10 Days Challenge! Decide how much you want to earn (could be exactly $10,000, could be more, could be less). Pick a start date. Assemble your cheerleading squad. And brainstorm a list of ways you're going to get that coin. The list on page 166 has some good ideas to get you started.

☐ Complete your $10k in 10 Days Challenge! Don't just plan it. Do it. Celebrate whatever amount you earned, whether it's exactly $10,000 or less or more. Every dollar is one dollar you didn't have before!

☐ Highly recommended: Open the book *We Should All Be Millionaires*. Read the chapter "A Million Dollar Now" to go even deeper into this topic.

☐ Fill in the blanks: "After completing the $10k in 10 Days Challenge, I feel _____

_____

_____

The biggest thing I learned is _____

_____

_____."

PUTTING IT ALL TOGETHER: YOUR MILLION DOLLAR PLAN

One final worksheet for you.

Pull together everything we've covered into a clear plan.

This plan represents your new attitude about money, and how you're going to live and work differently from this moment onward.

Million Dollar Story

From this moment forward, I will speak differently to myself. Instead of a Broke Ass Story about money, I will tell myself a Million Dollar Story that sounds like this:

I can _____

_____

_____

I am _____

_____

_____

Just like every other human being, I deserve _____

_____

_____

It is possible to _____

_____

_____

Million Dollar Lies

I understand that I've been fed lies about money (and my ability to earn it) from the media, the government, the patriarchy.

Oppressive systems have existed for a long time (since before I was born), and these systems have made it difficult for people like me to build wealth.

I've been told "If you struggle with money, that's all your fault," but this is a lie. I reject the lies I've been told. I won't let them poison my mind any longer.

I claim responsibility for _____

_____

_____

_____

_____

However, _____ is not my fault. I can release

responsibility for that _____

_____

_____

_____

I no longer believe _____

_____

_____

_____

_____

Million Dollar Decisions

I am ready to stop making Broke Ass Decisions and start making Million Dollar Decisions. The more MDDs I make, the faster my financial situation will change!

One Broke Ass Decision I will never make again: _____

_____

_____

_____

_____

One Million Dollar Decision I've already made: _____

_____

_____

_____

_____

Million Dollar Boundaries

I understand that setting a boundary means raising the standard for myself and others. Instead of settling for crumbs, or tolerating a crappy situation, I can raise the bar and set a new standard of living: "This is how it's going to be from now on." I acknowledge that boundaries are worthless unless they are enforced consistently.

One Million Dollar Boundary (new plan, new standard, new policy, exciting upgrade) I am making immediately: _____

_____

_____

_____

Million Dollar Squad

I realize that 95 percent of my success in life is determined by the people in my inner circle. I will surround myself with people who inspire me, and who bring financial and emotional riches into my life. I want to roll with people who've got a Million Dollar Attitude, so the golden money-dust can rub off on me!

One specific thing I will do to build my Million Dollar Squad and bring inspiring relationships into my life: _____

_____

_____

_____

_____

_____

Million Dollar Vision

I can't achieve a goal if I don't even know what the goal is. I recognize that I need to describe my Million Dollar Vision (my dream lifestyle) with clear, specific language. I need to clearly state where I want to live, what car I want to drive, all the details. And, I need to total it up to find out how much my dream life will actually cost.

My Million Dollar Vision includes (state at least five things your dream life includes): _____

_____

_____

_____

_____

_____

My Million Dollar Vision will cost approximately _____
per month. This is my new monthly income goal. I may not be earning that
much (yet) but I will get there.

One lifestyle upgrade that I can make immediately, so that I can start experiencing my Million Dollar Vision right now: _____

_____

_____

_____

_____

_____

_____

Million Dollar Value

*There is something I can do that is extremely valuable. It's important to identify my
"thing"—the skill, ability, or talent that has the potential to make me a whole lot of
money. Once I discover my "thing," I can unleash my inner millionaire badass and
those coins will rain down!*

One thing I can do that is extremely valuable: _____

_____

_____

_____

_____

I can make millions doing: _____

_____

_____

_____

_____

Million Dollar Pricing

I recognize that I have been under-earning my entire life. I could be earning exponentially more than I currently do.

No more charging peanuts or charging by the hour, which keeps my income limited to the hours in each day. From now on, I charge based on the value I provide. Even if I feel nervous to double my prices, I will face the fear and do it anyway.

My old price or salary: _____

My new price or salary: _____

Specific date when I will make this change: _____

Million Dollar Team

Nobody becomes a millionaire alone. Everyone needs a team, including me.

Even if I don't feel completely "ready" yet, I'm going to make my first hire. Whether it's a part-time personal assistant (or another role) I am building my Million Dollar Team now.

Having an assistant will free up hundreds of hours of my time over the next year. I will use that time to make millions.

First (or next) role I will hire: _____

_____

Specific date when this new team member will begin:

_____

Million Dollar Systems

If I feel disorganized and ashamed about my money, then I will struggle to earn more. It's time to get my house in order.

I'm excited to create financial systems to track my money and manage it thoughtfully, including scheduling Money Church (a date with me and my money) every week.

A few financial systems that I will set up immediately:

Specific date when this will be done:

My first Money Church session is scheduled for:

A Million Dollars Now

I can make a million excuses why "now is not the right time" to earn more money and build wealth. Or I can decide that now is exactly the right time.

I pledge to complete the $10k in 10 Days Challenge. I will find a way to bring an extra $10,000 into my bank account in ten days. It will be wild and exciting, it will push me to try some new things, and I am ready!

My $10k in 10 Days Challenge is happening soon, starting on:

To make $10,000, I will do the following things:

Once it's over, I will celebrate whatever amount of money I brought in the door (whether it's exactly $10,000, less, or more) and I will reward myself with:

IF
NOTHING
ELSE . . .

We're approaching the end of this workbook. We've covered a lot. You've been given quite a few action steps to do. Your mind might be feeling very full, so I want to strip things down and give you a few closing words to remember.

If you remember nothing else from this workbook, please remember the following words.

Take a photo of this page and the next. Underline text. Highlight things that feel especially relevant to you. These are the main points I want to plant firmly in your mind.

Always remember and never forget:

No matter who you are, or what you do for a living, you could be earning more than you currently do. There is always a way to bring more coin in the door.

You can start a side hustle that eventually grows into a full-time business with unlimited earning potential.

You can double your prices and start charging according to the value you provide, instead of charging by the hour.

You can scale your business by adding new team members so that your company can serve more clients and earn ten times your revenue.

You can negotiate a raise at work.

You can get a personal assistant who frees up twenty hours of your time every week, hundreds of hours every year, and then use that time to make millions.

You have the ability to earn more money whenever you want or need.

Your path to millionaire status will not look identical to mine. You have skills that I lack, and you face challenges I have never encountered. Each individual's path to wealth will be somewhat unique. That said, there are some universal money principles that apply to everyone, including you.

No matter who you are, you need to release your old money story if it's no longer serving you. You need to stop making Broke Ass Decisions and start making Million Dollar Decisions. You need to create a support network to keep you inspired and focused. You need to set up financial systems to track your money and stay organized.

Just like drinking water, getting sleep, and listening to whatever single Beyoncé just dropped, there are certain things that everyone must do.

I hope this workbook has outlined those must-do action steps for you very clearly. And I hope you will not just read them, but do them.

The last thing I want you to remember is this:

If you have struggled with money in the past, please stop blaming yourself.

Your money struggles are largely due to racist, misogynist, ableist, and homophobic systems that were designed to keep people like you broke, trapped, and disempowered.

Remember: Until fairly recently, women were not allowed to open a bank account, apply for a business loan, and many other wealth-building actions. We are lagging behind financially, and this is no accident. This is due to laws and other systems that forced us to stay behind.

Does this mean everything is hopeless and you are doomed to be financially stressed forever? No. But it does mean that you need to look at your financial situation from a different perspective and see your story in a new light.

You are not a frivolous person who spends too much and is bad with money.

You are a brave person who was born into a world that is grotesquely unjust. You are a hero who is striving to create wealth in spite of the obstacles in your path. You have decided to create millions despite starting with very little. You are making something out of practically nothing. You are someone to be admired, not shamed or chastised. I hope that you can begin to see yourself in this light. Because this is the truth.

When it comes to your financial situation, acknowledge the parts that are not your fault. There are so many things that are awful, unfair, and you didn't create those things. They existed long before you were born.

At the same time, take full responsibility for the parts that are within your control. Because there are actually a lot of things that you can control. You can take charge of your boundaries, your pricing, your systems. You have a great deal of power. Use it.

The path to wealth is paved with Million Dollar Decisions. Make one Million Dollar Decision today. Then another. And another. Keep going. You will be astonished by how much your life changes in one month or one year.

Stay the course.

Get that coin.

NOTES

CONCLUSION

t's one thing to know, "I need to drink more water, eat vegetables, and take a walk." It's another thing to actually do it. Knowing is great. Doing is how you see and feel results.

And, of course, this applies to your money. It's one thing to know, "I could be earning more," "I could raise my prices," "I need to set boundaries to protect my time." It is another thing to actually do those steps.

I hope this workbook has provided you with specific Million Dollar Actions to do and sufficient motivation to go do them.

Even if you complete just 10 percent of the Million Dollar Actions in the workbook, that alone will begin to change your financial situation. If you do 100 percent of the steps, even better.

If you find yourself struggling to take action, get curious about *why*. "What is stopping me from doing the things I know I need to do?" "Why do I keep resisting, procrastinating, or avoiding this work?" "What do I need in order to clear these blocks out of the way?"

You may need more than a workbook and a pen. You may need professional help from a coach, counselor, therapist, or trauma expert. Identify the support you need and give it to yourself. No block is permanent and all blocks can be cleared.

To circle back to the very beginning of this workbook, allow me to remind you once again about my all-time hero: Madam C. J. Walker. She became the first female millionaire in the United States more than a hundred years ago. If she could do it then, you can do it now. And you should.

We should all follow in Walker's footsteps, and other visionaries like her.

We should all charge more, earn more, have more, especially those of us who have been marginalized and denied even the most basic financial rights for hundreds of years.

We should all have a safe and comfortable home, healthy food in the fridge, and plenty of savings for unexpected events.

We should all have a surplus of money so we can donate to causes that matter and repair the systems that are so terribly broken.

We should all have enough cash to graduate with a bachelor's, master's, or doctorate debt-free, if we so choose, and enable our kids to do the same.

We should all get to experience, at least once, the joy of paying off a mortgage in full and owe absolutely nothing.

We should all live in peace, without financial stress hovering in the fringes of every waking moment and disrupting our sleep.

We should all know what it feels like to wake up and see seven zeroes in our bank account, and feel what it's like to wield that kind of economic power.

We should all be able to live a beautiful quality of life and die with no regrets, knowing that our loved ones are provided for, and more than enough is left behind, a legacy for those still alive.

We should all be emotionally, spiritually, and financially rich.

We should all be millionaires.

NOTES

_____

_____

_____

_____

_____

_____

_____

_____

_____

_____

_____

ADDITIONAL RESOURCES

EVERY DAY: DO THE DAILY SEVEN

Want to become a millionaire? Do these seven action steps—every day—to generate more money and more time, energy, peace, power, and joy. Make these seven things a nonnegotiable part of your daily routine.

Today and Every Day

1. Delegate one task on your to-do list to someone else.

Assign a task to an employee, to your partner or spouse, to somebody you hire on TaskRabbit.com, to your teenager, to the ex that you co-parent with, or someone else. Clear something off your plate and lighten your load.

2. Move your body.

Go for a walk, swing a kettlebell, do a yoga class, twerk, swim, stretch, do tai chi. Do anything that feels loving to your body. Just move.

3. Connect with your squad.

Call a friend. Send a text. Pop a note in the mail. Log on to an online community (like We Should All Be Millionaires: The Club, or another network you're in) and tell someone about a goal you're working on, or give a pep talk to someone else and make that person's day. We're only as strong as the relationships in our lives.

4. Do one money-generating activity.

A money-generating activity is any action step that brings money in the door, either immediately or in the very near future.

Examples include:

- Email a potential client and invite that person to hire you,

- Ask your boss for a raise, bonus, or profit-sharing arrangement,

- Nudge a client to pay an invoice that's overdue,

- Sell clothes or furniture that you don't want,

- Ask your cousin to pay back the money you loaned him in 2007,

- Raise your prices and charge based on the value you provide,

- Send a newsletter to your mailing list to announce your new program and invite people to enroll,

- Notify family and friends about your new side hustle and ask them to keep you in mind and send clients to you,

- Submit your tax return so you can get that refund you're owed,

- Bop off a press release to the media to announce your new product,

- Or anything else that brings cash into your bank account.

Do something every day to generate resources: money, as well as time, energy, and opportunities.

5. Think million dollar thoughts.

Remind yourself that you are smart, resourceful, and capable of generating money. You've done challenging things in the past and you can do this, too.

Feed yourself thoughts that make you feel powerful.

6. Look at your money.

How much money do you have? What's happening with it? Are you spending money in alignment with your values—spending on the people you love and the causes you care about? Or is something raggedy goin' on?

Notice your money. Pay attention to it. Feel gratitude for every dollar you've got (even if it isn't much right now!) and send love to your bank account.

You can feel deep gratitude and be ambitious and hungry for more . . . at the same time.

7. Set or enforce a boundary.

Setting a boundary means: raising the standards in terms of how you allow people to treat you.

You allow your kids to interrupt you while you're trying to work and make money? That stops today.

You exhaust yourself cooking dinner while your spouse enjoys a nice nap? No, ma'am.

You allow your boss or top client to pester you with "urgent emails" at 7:00 p.m. on a Friday night and weekends, too? Not anymore.

Choose one area of your life where you've settled for bullshit or tolerated a whole lot of nonsense and do something about it. Set a boundary. Enforce a rule. Raise the standards. Today.

Your Daily Seven Checklist

☐ Delegate one task on your to-do list to someone else. What did you delegate today?

_____

_____

_____

_____

_____

☐ Move your body. How did you move your body today?

_____

_____

_____

_____

_____

☐ Connect with your squad. How did you connect with your peeps today? Did you reach out to a couple of people? Or to one person in particular? Who?

☐ Do one money-generating activity. What's the MGA that you did today—and what happened? Did it pay off immediately? Will it pay off in the near future? Do you feel proud that you did it?

☐ Think million dollar thoughts. What's a powerful thought or statement that you said to yourself today?

☐ Look at your money. How did you bring attention to your money today? Log in to check your online banking? Glance at your retirement funds? Peek at your budget? Count all the bills in your wallet? What did you do today?

_____

_____

_____

_____

☐ Set or enforce a boundary. Choose one area of your life where you've been settling for crumbs and do something about it. Raise the standards. Demand more of others—or yourself. What's the boundary you set or enforced today?

_____

_____

_____

_____

PS. Love this Daily Seven Checklist? Head to helloseven.co/daily7 to get a digital/ PDF version of the checklist that you can print at home. Print seven copies. Then, pledge to do the Daily Seven for seven days in a row. Notice how different you feel after one week.

EVERY WEEK: GO TO MONEY CHURCH

What is Money Church and how does it work?

Inside We Should All Be Millionaires: The Club (an online community for marginalized people who want to make bank), we have a monthly session called Money Church.

Even if you aren't a member of We Should All Be Millionaires: The Club, you can still do your own personal Money Church every week . . . and we highly recommend that you do.

To be clear: Money Church is not about worshipping money. Money Church is a weekly, pleasurable date with your money. Carve out a sixty- or ninety-minute time slot in your calendar when you will not be distracted. Use this time for Money Church.

During the time you've blocked out . . .

1. Look at your money.

Log in to your online banking or look at your money-tracking software or spreadsheets. Even if you only have $10 in your checking account right now, it's powerful to bring attention to your money and look toward it instead of looking away.

2. Go over the numbers.

How much do you currently have sitting in the bank? How much is flowing in soon? Do you have potential money that is likely but not confirmed yet—like a client who wants to hire you but hasn't officially made a deposit? And, how much is flowing out?

3. Review your books and your latest bookkeeping reports.

This includes examining the financial decisions you've made recently. For instance: hiring a personal assistant, raising your prices, selling a car, and so on. What are some Broke Ass Decisions you've made lately? What are some Million Dollar Decisions you've made, too? Forgive yourself for the BAD moves—learn, let go, and move on. Celebrate your wins.

4. Write down any patterns you notice and personal "aha" moments you have after looking at the numbers.

5. Spend some time examining your limiting beliefs.

What's a Broke Ass Story you have been telling yourself lately? Examine those thoughts and reframe them into more helpful, positive thoughts.

6. Use your remaining time to brainstorm new moneymaking ideas and set financial goals.

Recommendation: write down at least twenty-five ideas you have for making more money every week. You don't necessarily need to do all these things. But, try to expand your thinking and come up with as many possibilities as you can.

7. Come up with exciting rewards to motivate yourself to get moving.

Think of how you will reward yourself once you execute one of these moneymaking ideas. For example, your goal might be "I'm going to get three new clients for my dog-walking service this month." And the reward might be "Once I get these three clients, I am going to reward myself with those new running sneakers I've been eyeing."

_____

_____

_____

_____

Do those seven things to have a very successful Money Church session.

Do Money Church alone or do it with a friend, significant other, business partner, or a group of people.

Enjoy your first Money Church session, hopefully the first of many! Do it weekly. Make this a regular, nonnegotiable part of your financial routine. Watch your prosperity increase tenfold.

EVERY YEAR: DO AN ANNUAL MONEY REVIEW

What is an Annual Money Review?

It's a chance to look at your money, think about your money, get cozy with your money, snuggle up to it, love on it, have a date with it.

And it's an opportunity to reflect on how the last year went and take a moment of gratitude for the money you've got (even if it's not that much . . . yet).

Set aside a few hours to do your Annual Money Review. Give yourself enough time to settle in so you don't feel rushed.

Light a candle. Play peaceful music to set the mood. Clear your desk and your mind. Bring your undivided attention. Make this moment feel inspiring and important, like a date with someone you care about. Your Annual Money

Review is like an extra-special Money Church session where you review the whole year, not just the last week.

To complete your Annual Money Review, answer the following ten questions.

1. What is one Million Dollar Decision you made in the last year?

A Million Dollar Decision is any decision that generates more money, expands your life, creates more options, or brings you time, energy, peace, power, and joy.

A Million Dollar Decision could be launching a new business, hiring a personal assistant, or getting a haircut that doubles your confidence.

Write down your favorite Million Dollar Decision from the last year. If you made tons of Million Dollar Decisions, amazing, make a big list! Celebrate these wins.

2. What is one Broke Ass Decision you made in the last year?

A Broke Ass Decision is any decision that costs you money, constricts your life, eliminates options and makes you feel stuck and trapped, steals your time, depletes you in any way, or simply makes you feel like crap.

A Broke Ass Decision could be agreeing to work with a disrespectful client who sucks the light out of your eyes, undercharging for your services or working for free, or allowing your kids to interrupt you constantly while you're trying to get that paper.

Did you make some Broke Ass Decisions this year that depleted you financially, emotionally, or both? Make a list.

_____

_____

_____

_____

_____

_____

_____

_____

_____

_____

Reflect. Forgive yourself. Move on. We're definitely not doing that again.

3. How much money did you generate in the last year?

Add up all the money you brought in the door—money you earned from your job or business, money you earned from investing, money you generated by doing a garage sale or starting a side hustle, any money you brought in the door.

What's the grand total?

And, what's the average per month?

_____

_____

_____

_____

_____

_____

_____

4. What's one area of your financial life where you feel messy, disorganized, ashamed, or just not very confident?

   For instance, maybe you haven't looked at your credit card balance in
   months because you don't want to see "the big number."

   Or maybe you don't have a legit system for organizing receipts and tracking business expenses—you just stuff everything into the Shoebox of Shame
   and hide it in the closet.

   What's not feeling good?

_____

_____

_____

_____

_____

_____

5. Think about the messy situation that you just wrote down. What are you
   going to do about this?

   What's your plan? You will feel so much better when you deal with it instead of avoiding the situation. So, what do you need to do?

Do you need to hire a bookkeeper, accountant, tax expert, business coach, financial planner, personal assistant, attorney, or someone else?

Or is there something else you need to do? A system you need to create? How are you going to grow up and glow up?

_____

_____

_____

_____

_____

6. What is your net worth?

Your net worth is everything you own—minus what you owe.

Add up all the money you have: everything in your checking, savings, and retirement account(s). Then add the value of everything you own: home, land, car, boat, fine art, jewelry, anything else you own. Do you have any other assets? Add those, too.

Find the grand total of everything you have/own. Then subtract any debt you owe—credit card debt, student loan debt, real estate mortgage you haven't paid off yet, and so on.

What are you left with?

_____

_____

_____

_____

_____

Right now, your net worth might be $26.14. It might be $100,000. It might be $-80,000, if you have more debt than assets right now.

Whatever the number is, know that it's only a temporary position. This is where you are, right now. This is not necessarily where you are going to be in six months, one year, or three years. But it's important to look at the number and know where you stand, rather than burying your head in the sand.

7. What is your dream lifestyle—and how much would it actually cost to have that life?

For instance, if you want to live in a three-bedroom, three-bathroom home in the best 'hood in town, drive a Lexus, have a nanny for your kids, a personal assistant, a house cleaner who comes twice a week, a personal chef who handles dinner on weeknights, excellent health insurance coverage, and everything else you desire, how much would that cost? Hint: Google can tell you everything you need to know.

Write down everything your dream life includes. Make a list. Then do the math. Figure out how much you need to have your dream situation. Get a monthly number. Is it $10,000 per month? $15,000? $25,000? $50,000? More? It doesn't have to be exact. Ballpark is fine. Now you know what you're aiming for: your new monthly income target.

Even if you've done this exercise before, do it again. Because the dream life you envisioned one year ago may be different from your vision today. The details and numbers may have changed.

8. How could you generate the money you need?

If your dream life costs $25,000 per month, what's your plan to reach that number? Brainstorm twenty-five ways you could bring money in the door. Write down serious ideas and ridiculous, wild notions too

You don't need to do all twenty-five things. The goal here is to expand your thinking and come up with fresh ideas.

9. What is the old money attitude that you are leaving behind?

Example: I am terrible with money. I have so much debt. I will never be wealthy.

_____

_____

_____

_____

_____

_____

_____

_____

10. What is the new money attitude that you are bringing into the next year?

Example: I am smart and resourceful. I can generate more money whenever I want or need to. I can change my financial situation. Other women have done this, and I can do it, too.

_____

_____

_____

_____

_____

_____

_____

_____

Congratulations! You officially completed your Annual Money Review.

Go pop the bubbly, blast some music, and treat yourself to something you really want (whether it costs money or not).

Very few people take the time to sit down and complete an Annual Money Review. Most people avoid looking at their money and don't want to discuss it or even think about it—because it feels too uncomfortable or scary.

The fact that you completed this review signals that you are serious about earning more money, and you're not afraid to put in the work. Congrats, and don't stop now. Keep rising.

SURPRISE!

We Should All Be Millionaires: The Club is an online community with more than two thousand people who all share one goal: making more money and becoming a thriving, wealthy badass.

This is a diverse community comprised of women, people of color, queer folks, and other people who aren't traditionally welcomed into conversations about wealth.

We call our Club members "Shmillies." That's short for Shmillionaire. (Shout out to Cardi B!)

We told our Shmillies, "Hey! We're making a workbook." And we asked them, "Imagine there are people out there who want to make more money but feel overwhelmed. They are struggling to get moving and take action. What would you like to say to them? Please share one piece of advice, or something you feel they need to hear."

The Shmillies came through . . . big time. There was an outpouring of advice, encouragement, and profound love and care for you: the person reading this right now.

We pulled together a few statements (surprise!), and here they are. We hope this lifts your spirits and reminds you that other people have changed their financial situation, and you can do it, too.

Here's what the Shmillies wanted to say . . . to you.

Women, in particular, have systemically been taught to dim our own light. Not be "too" anything: too loud, too smart, too pretty, too outgoing, too available. And we have internalized all of that. This was the most difficult part of starting a business for me. To shed the opinions and expectations of others and stand in the story I am writing for myself. We have believed others for far too long and played so small in doing so. Get out of your own way and see how bright you can shine.

—CARMEN CERVANTES

We have been conditioned to be grateful for what we have, to believe it is all we are worthy of. You are allowed to THRIVE, you hear me? Your job in this life is not simply to survive. YOU are allowed to ask for more than what you need. When YOU win, we all do. So shoot for the big, audacious dream, make a plan, and then get to work. The life you dream of is on the other side of the scary action you've been avoiding. You are more than ready.

—MARIANGELICA FORERO

The best thing I have learned is to "do it ugly." I realized that is how I moved up in my business so quickly and I need to keep telling myself that as I keep moving up. The biggest reason why we don't move is because we are afraid we will make a mistake. When you truly put yourself first and your million dollar vision you aren't making a mistake. You are learning from your mistakes. —MICHELLE KAIS

Overwhelm comes from overcomplicating things! The most powerful tool you hold is your voice! Society has benefited from telling us to "quiet down, speak softer, don't speak unless you're spoken to." And even then, we're made to feel bad for what it is we have to say. You have a message inside of you to speak, share, and serve into the world! Take the time to recenter yourself within your voice and fullest expression. What is something you CAN share into the world right now? It may come to you so naturally, that you question if it's "too easy or too simple." That's just called your genius gift! Own that! Start with that! Show up for that! Shine in that! Get the clarity you need to share that into the world with the people who most need and want it and watch money become less and less overwhelming! But it starts with you unlocking and unleashing your message within. Expand your mind, expand your message, expand your money! Each of us have a message and genius gift meant to be used to up-level our own life so go monetize your message and impact others! Let it be easy love, it's your time to show up and shine in your power message! Because the money is always in the message! —KIERRA JONES

Remember that the greatest return on investment you'll ever receive is the investment you make in you. You may be thinking, Can I do this? and the answer is "yes" but only if you take the first step and then the next step after that. One of the biggest mistakes we make as entrepreneurs is allowing fear and perfectionism to hold us back, but there so much power in the messy middle. That's where the true CEO in you is birthed, so cheers to taking the first step and doing it scared. You got this. I believe in you. Now it's your turn. Let's get it.
—AHFEEYAH C. THOMAS-SALOMON

We oftentimes say that we have faith but don't act in it. Faith isn't waiting until the door opens to walk through, faith is walking through knowing the door will open.
—TISH WARE

Your brilliance is absolutely extraordinary to others. Why not take everything that's wrapped around your finger and give it to others? This is the starting place to launch your business. Belief that people need what you have. You'll quickly find out you can live your purpose AND achieve wealth. We do it together, shoulder to shoulder. Here's the baton; come on in and build your business. —DORA RANKIN

Delegation maximizes your time, your impact, your joy and thus your life. Delegate more and often. You are worthy of joy, peace, and prosperity.
—ELISE BUIE

For far too long, society has put disabled people in an impossibly tiny box. We are told to keep ourselves small, because we're disabled, after all. We are told we cannot obtain wealth, or get married, lest we lose our chances at receiving support. I say, we are done being brought to heel and done accepting the narrative that disabled people cannot be wealthy, or that we are less than. You are inherently *valuable, and the world needs your gifts. It's time to let go of who society thinks you should be, and embrace who you know you are: an absolute force for change.*

—DAISY MONTGOMERY

If you want to become a millionaire, focus on the art of transformation and self-seduction, a.k.a. self-love. Until you're willing to show up for yourself and release old trauma, you'll rely on your clients and potential clients to be your emotional surrogates. Until you focus on your self-love journey, you won't trust people like Rachel to guide you. You are worthy, and the world needs you. Now, get out there and make this money so you can truly change the world. Pow! —PERLE NOIRE

Advocate for yourself! You are entitled to an abundant life and that calling inside your heart needs to be answered. Abolish the generational scarcity mindset that has been passed down and step into your power. Perfection leads to procrastination, launch it ugly and have self-compassion. You are worthy of all the good things life has to offer! —CANDY DIAZ

To be that successful entrepreneur, you need to stay focused on your why . . . because the road to becoming a millionaire is like a roller coaster ride of a lot highs and lows. Consistency, dedication, perseverance, and focus are the key attributes to that success. —ELIS FERNANDEZ PAYNE

Money will not change the world by itself, but paired with your values, it really can. Letting yourself set the boundaries you need, to truly allow this to work out, is an enormous, courageous, and chain-breaking step. Your future beneficiaries will thank you for everything you're preparing to face. —MEGAN MELLIN

Money is a tool, not the end goal. Find your purpose, create value, and the wealth will follow. Focus on impact, and the rest will fall into place. —MIA SELPH

Pause. Look around. Focus on what you have, not what you think you are missing. Then, close your eyes and go within and say thank you. The more gratitude you give the more that comes into your life to be grateful for.

—BARBARA VALENZUELA

To every woman reading this, understand that your core, your "I AM," is a potent force. Embrace it, cherish it, and let it lead you from the maze of sorrow to the expansive meadows of abundance. Your mind will align, and your body will naturally yearn for sacred self-care. Our narratives aren't mere survival tales; they are powerful songs of triumphant resurgence. By distinguishing religion from spirituality, I had an epiphany: abundance was my innate right, and then I was ready to fully embrace it.

—DAISY JONES-BROWN

The number one thing that took my business and bank account to the next level was FOCUS. As a creative, the fear of missing out is so real. You think you have to do all the things at the same time. But, in actuality, this fear will keep you stuck, and you will find yourself in the same place year after year. However, when you decide to focus, you will indeed FLOURISH. And your future self will thank you for it.

—DAARINA FAROOQ-JANNAH

Just take the very next step. You may not know where exactly it will lead or what's on the other side. But just take that step. The next step may look like talking to someone to gain more clarity. It may look like creating an exit plan from a time, energy, or money sucking situation. It may look like talking to everyone you know about what you've been up to. If you can dream it, it is for you to have, so let's do it!

—TANITRA SCORZA

Let's get this out of the way: YOU WILL MAKE MISTAKES. Some might even be big. But let's also get this straight: you can handle this. Trust yourself. Trust your resources. Trust that whatever decision you make and however it ends you can figure it out. Actions are your choices made real. Action is the activator in your perm. Action is the eggs in your cake. Action is the gas in your car. Action is the ingredient that makes it all come together. Send that invoice and run away if you have to, but send the invoice. Hit post and close your laptop, but hit post. Schedule a call when you're *almost* ready, but schedule that call. Do it scared. Do it screaming with your eyes closed, but do it.

—TAMAY SHANNON

No one can be you like you. Honor your needs and protect the boundaries that allow you to keep showing up as your uniquely wonderful self. These habits are what will attract the most aligned people and opportunities to you. Also, lean into those dreams and visions that scare you a bit; they will eventually lead you to your deepest desires and breakthroughs. —VANESSA BELLAMY

Borrow courage from your past to feed the courage you need to face today's fears. —MONIQUE VALASQUEZ

Start before you feel ready. Feeling ready and being ready are two different things, and feelings lie. If you have the dream in your heart, you are ready to take the next step. —JEAN ALI MUHLBAUER

Do it together. Find people to grow with and you'll supercharge your trajectory and you'll have a lot more fun, too. —CHRISTINA KIFFNEY

Money is a tool. What do you want to do with that tool? Having more of it doesn't make you a "bad" or "greedy" person. It is all about what you do with it and how you use it to build out your dream life. —CAROLINE TANIS

MILLION DOLLAR IDEAS

Enjoy these blank pages.

Write down Million Dollar Ideas that pop into your brain. Draw a picture of your future wallet, stuffed with cash. Make a list of business ideas. Anything you want to do.

WE SHOULD ALL BE MILLIONAIRES: THE CLUB

- Clear the mental blocks that hold you back from earning more money.

- Discover moneymaking options that you'd never considered before.

- Shift from knowing to doing, and take steps to increase your income by 30 percent (minimum) within the next twelve months.

- Get inspired by smart, ambitious people who are making moves and raking in the coins. See what they're doing, how they're doing it, and get inspired. Let the golden money-dust rub off on you!

- Chat with expert money coaches, available to answer questions and give you a push whenever you need it.

It's all happening inside We Should All Be Millionaires: The Club.

This Club is online. Participate from anywhere in the world. Any country. Any time zone. Women, people of color, queer folks: this Club is a safe and inclusive place where you are celebrated and where you'll find people like you.

We have one goal: to help you earn exponentially more than you currently do. Learn more and become a member at helloseven.co/club.

Hang out with us and you will make more money. Guaranteed.

Club Members Say . . .

I don't know where I would be without Rachel Rodgers and this amazing community she has cocreated.
                                                    —NICOLE BARHAM

Joining the Club was one of the best investments I've made in my personal and professional life. Not only has it helped me make a LOT more money and have better systems in place so I can have more ease in my life, but it also has been a really great way for me to make friends and colleagues that are on my level.

—LAUREN MARIE FLEMING

I have done so many business courses, and none have affected me and my work like this. Very grateful.

—MARTHA BOURLAKAS

BECOME A CERTIFIED
HELLO SEVEN COACH

- Teach diverse entrepreneurs how to grow a business from zero to seven figures and beyond.

- Support clients as they achieve exciting financial goals and build generational wealth.

- Help clients shift from overworking, under-earning, and financial stress to prosperity.

- Get paid to change lives, families, and communities.

WHAT IS A HELLO SEVEN COACH?

A Hello Seven Coach is a business coach + money coach + mindset coach—all in one.

You work with diverse entrepreneurs: women, BIPOC, LGBTQIA, and people with disabilities—entrepreneurs with huge potential who are under-estimated and underserved.

You help each client change their attitude about money, achieve financial goals, build a successful business, and create generational wealth.

You teach each client the proprietary trademarked Hello Seven Method—a step-by-step path to grow a business from $0 to $100k to $1,000,000 and beyond. Goodbye, scarcity. Hello, seven figures.

You can coach part-time or full-time, in person or online, work with clients one-on-one or in groups, the options are unlimited. Your work as a Hello Seven Coach can be anything you want it to be.

WHY WE NEED MORE
HELLO SEVEN COACHES . . . NOW

There is a severe power imbalance in our world.

White cisgender heterosexual men control the vast majority of the world's wealth.

Women, BIPOC, LGBTQIA, and people with disabilities earn crumbs in comparison.

- For every dollar a white man earns, women earn less. White women: 79 cents. Black women: 62 cents. Native American women: 57 cents. Latina women: 54 cents. [US Bureau of Labor]

- Women own 51 percent of all businesses in the United States but only bring in 4 percent of the revenue. [Amex State of Women Owned Businesses Report]

- Women are 80 percent more likely than men to be impoverished in retirement. [National Institute on Retirement Security]

- A Black household in America has an average net worth of $17,000. White household: $170,000. [Pew Research]

- Nearly 30 percent of bisexual women and 23 percent of lesbians (ages 18–44) live in poverty. [The Williams Institute]

- Full-time, year-round workers with a disability earn 87 cents for every dollar earned by those with no disability. [US Census]

- 90 percent of the world's millionaires are men. Only 10 percent are women. [GlobalData Wealth Insight]

As long as this wealth gap exists, we will never have equity, justice, and fairness in our world.

At Hello Seven, our mission is to close the gap—one entrepreneur at a time.

We have served more than 10,000 clients—and 10,000 is only the beginning. We want to reach millions more so that we can create massive change.

To do that, we need more Hello Seven Coaches.

IDEAL CANDIDATE

We're looking for a particular kind of person, and it might be you.
Criteria:

- You want to learn a highly marketable skill that can make you a millionaire.

- You want to help people set exciting financial goals and achieve them.

- You want to learn more about entrepreneurship and money.

- You have an encouraging personality. When people spend time with you, they feel capable and leave thinking, "I can do this."

- You feel called to work with women, BIPOC, LGBTQIA, people with disabilities, and/or other historically excluded communities.

- You want to help people break out of the painful cycle of over-working, under-earning, and financial stress.

- You want to learn how to take a business from zero to seven figures and beyond, and teach others how to do the same.

- You want to clear your own personal money blocks, build a million dollar mindset, and help your clients do this too.

- You can envision yourself coaching part-time or full-time and want to get paid to do this.

- You are frustrated by the wealth gap in our society and want to do something to fix it.

APPLY

If that's you, apply to become a Hello Seven Coach at helloseven.co/coach.

ABOUT THE AUTHOR

RACHEL RODGERS is the founder and CEO of Hello Seven, a multimillion-dollar company that teaches diverse entrepreneurs how to earn more money and build wealth. Hello Seven has been recognized as one of the fastest growing private companies in America by *Inc. Magazine* for the past three years.

Rachel's mission is to teach historically excluded groups how to end the cycle of overworking, under-earning, and financial stress once and for all, and to build generational wealth.

Rachel is the founder of We Should All Be Millionaires: The Club, an online network for diverse professionals that has helped hundreds become millionaires and thousands become financially free. Her debut book, *We Should All Be Millionaires: A Woman's Guide to Earning More, Building Wealth, and Gaining Economic Power* (HarperCollins Leadership) is a *WSJ*, *USA Today*, and Amazon Best Seller.

She is also the founder of the Hello Seven Foundation, which provides doula and childcare services to Black mothers in need, free of charge. As well as other services that help close the racial and gender wealth gaps.

You can find Rachel hosting *The Hello Seven Podcast* and sharing her visionary guidance in places like *Good Morning America*, *The New York Times*, *The Drew Barrymore Show*, *Forbes*, *Entrepreneur*, *Inc.*, *Women's Health*, and *The Tamron Hall Show*.